Praise for *Life and Lobster*

"Cousins Maine Lobster is the best investment I've made and one of the smartest businesses I've seen."

—Barbara Corcoran, Star, ABC's *Shark Tank*

"This isn't a story of overnight success. It's a story of conviction and endurance because growth in business is messy, uncertain, and hard-won."

—Robert Herjavec, Bestselling Author and Star, ABC's *Shark Tank*

"An unusually candid portrait of what it takes to build a food business that lasts. This is entrepreneurship as it actually happens."

—Danny Meyer, Restaurateur and Author, *Setting the Table* and *The Transforming Power of Hospitality in Business*

LIFE AND LOBSTER

LIFE AND LOBSTER

From *Shark Tank* to a Billion-Dollar Business

(and How We Almost Lost It All)

SABIN LOMAC and JIM TSELIKIS

MATT HOLT

Matt Holt Books
An Imprint of BenBella Books, Inc.
Dallas, TX

The events, locations and conversations in this book, while true, are re-created from the author's memory. However, the essence of the story and the feelings and emotions evoked are intended to be accurate representations. In certain instances, names, persons, organizations, and places have been changed to protect an individual's privacy.

MATT HOLT BENBELLA

Matt Holt is an imprint of BenBella Books, Inc.
BenBella Books, Inc.
8080 N. Central Expressway
Suite 1700
Dallas, TX 75206
benbellabooks.com
Send feedback to feedback@benbellabooks.com

Matt Holt and *BenBella* are federally registered trademarks.

Printed in the United States of America
10 9 8 7 6 5 4 3 2 1

Library of Congress Control Number: 2026016052
ISBN 9781637749784 (hardcover)
ISBN 9781637749791 (electronic)

Editing by Stephanie Gorton
Copyediting by Scott Calamar
Proofreading by Martha Gallant and Rebecca Maines
Text design and composition by PerfecType, Nashville, TN
Cover design by Jason Arias
Cover photo © Heidi Kirn
Printed by Lake Book Manufacturing

Jim:

To my parents, thank you for raising me the right way. I love you.

To my daughters, Olive and Coco. You are my world.

Smile always, and dream big. I love you.

To Maggie, I love you most. Only Once. GBAW

Sabin:

To Erika, Enzo, and Isla. I love you.

CONTENTS

FOREWORD

People love to romanticize entrepreneurship.

They see the headlines, the exits, the shiny moments on social media. They see "overnight success," not the ten years of grinding that came before it. What they don't see are the doubts you swallow, the debt you juggle, the rejection you pretend doesn't sting. They don't see the quiet nights when you bet on yourself and wonder if you just made the biggest mistake of your life.

That's exactly why this book matters.

What Sabin Lomac and Jim Tselikis built with Cousins Maine Lobster didn't begin as a brand. It didn't start with national attention, and it definitely didn't start with a *Shark Tank* deal. It began the way most real businesses do: with grit and a belief that refused to die.

When they walked into the Tank, they didn't come in with a perfectly polished pitch. They came in with a real story and a product they stood behind with everything they had. Barbara made the deal that day, but I walked out as a genuine fan. Not just of the lobster rolls, but of the way these guys think and operate.

Mindset is the real business. Everything else is a tool.

This book isn't a highlight reel or a blueprint wrapped in academic language. There's no guaranteed formula here. What you're about to read is their unfiltered truth. The kind of truth that only comes from being in the trenches when nobody is clapping for you yet.

Sabin and Jim never let themselves be defined by what they lacked. No fancy degrees. No easy shortcuts. No playbook written by someone with different values and a different life. What they had was hunger, conviction, and the willingness to bet on themselves when sitting still would've been far easier.

Most people want the inspiration. Few want the discomfort that creates it.

I know that from experience. Before FUBU was anything, before *Shark Tank*, before any of the titles or accolades, I was just a kid from Queens sewing hats at my mother's house. No money. No safety net. Plenty of people telling me all the ways it would never work. I learned early that your belief has to drown out their opinions if you plan to get anywhere.

Sabin and Jim figured that out too.

They didn't wait for permission. They didn't look for validation. They trusted the lessons they learned growing up, the instincts that came from real life—not a textbook. They acted. They adjusted. They kept moving.

That's the line between entrepreneurs and spectators: action over intention.

This book pulls the curtain back on what it actually looks like to build something from scratch. The wrong turns. The ugly parts. The moments when quitting makes more logical sense than continuing. The times when fear feels louder than ambition.

But hidden inside those moments is where the real transformation happens.

Entrepreneurship isn't clean or predictable. It's messy, emotional, risky, and deeply personal. The folks who make it aren't the ones who have the most resources. They're the ones who refuse to tap out when the process gets uncomfortable.

What I admire most about Sabin and Jim is that they didn't try to imitate anyone. They didn't chase some polished version of success. They built something that reflected *them*: their values, their voice, their vision. They created a brand and a lifestyle that didn't exist before. And in doing that, they created proof.

Proof that opportunity can come from anywhere. Proof that you don't need titles to build something meaningful. Proof that real education comes from rolling up your sleeves. Proof that belief plus work is still the most powerful combination in business.

This foreword isn't about the deal we didn't make. It's about the mindset we share.

The mindset that says:

"I don't know everything, but I'll learn."
"I'm not fully ready, but I'm starting anyway."
"I'm scared, but I'm still moving."

People wait for perfect timing, perfect information, perfect confidence. That moment never shows up. The winners are the ones who move in spite of the uncertainty.

As you read this book, understand something: This isn't just a story about lobster rolls or food trucks or scaling a company. It's a story about ownership. Ownership of your decisions, your discipline, your vision. It's about carrying the weight of a dream when nobody else can see it yet.

You're about to get a front-row seat to what it really costs to build something that lasts.

And if you're an entrepreneur (or someone thinking about becoming one) I hope you get two things out of this book.

First, I hope it kills the illusion. The fantasy is what sets people up for disappointment.

Second, I hope it frees you to be imperfect. To start unpolished. To learn as you go. To build from where you are, not where you wish you were.

Because that's how real businesses are born.

Sabin and Jim didn't win because everything went smoothly. They won because they kept going when it didn't. They took hits. They adjusted. They kept swinging.

That's entrepreneurship. And that's the road you're about to walk with them.

If parts of this book make you uncomfortable, that's a good sign. Growth usually does. If it challenges the way you think, even better. If it makes you question whether you're playing too small, then it's already succeeded.

I'm proud of what these guys built. I'm proud of how they built it. And I'm excited for what their story will unlock for every builder and dreamer who picks up this book.

Turn the page.

The real story starts here.

—Daymond John

INTRODUCTION

Not many people can pinpoint the precise day and time their lives were irrevocably changed forever.* We can: 8 PM (Eastern Standard Time), October 19, 2012, with the broadcast of episode 6, season 4 of *Shark Tank*.

Indeed, it is likely that if you're leafing through these pages in a bookstore, it's because you've spotted the shot of the vaguely familiar guys on the cover.

But be forewarned: This will not be the version of us or our story you probably expect.

We get that. In the rearview mirror, our company, Cousins Maine Lobster, looks to have always been destined for success. Talk about a can't-miss formula: Great idea. Terrific product. Perfect timing. And that's *before* the titanic boost right out of the gate afforded by our appearance on a major national TV show.

Okay, no false modesty here, it also didn't hurt that we are sometimes described as good-looking, and—how to put this?—embodying

* Okay, excepting victims of tragedies or natural disasters. If by chance you lived in Pompeii, for instance, and survived the eruption of Mount Vesuvius, you probably didn't forget what happened a little past 1 PM on August 24, 79 AD.

a kind of casual, blue-collar manliness. (We don't think of ourselves that way—at least, one of us doesn't—but, hey, anything for the cause.)

Anyway, what we're getting at is that this is NOT your typical how-to-succeed story. To the contrary, it is a story—and one we suspect is of far greater universal application—of how, despite all we had going for us, we came close to NOT succeeding. How we royally screwed up and almost fucking blew it.

So in large part it is a tale of naïveté leading to unforced errors and jaw-dropping blunders. A blueprint, in short, of the sorts of mistakes every would-be entrepreneur should be sure to not make.

But it is also about how to recover if they get made anyway—how to wise up, keep going, and fight your way out of it.

In other words, it is the story of the all-important X factor: the hearts and minds of those who survive and prosper, as opposed to those who don't. Because bad things—and bad people—will happen to almost everyone with the guts to trade security for a leap into the wilds of the free market.

In our case, that leap seemed especially reckless. Both of us were leaving behind thriving careers we enjoyed, working alongside people we liked and esteemed. And for what?

A *food truck.*

The odds were infinitely greater that we'd end up flat broke on our asses than that this lunatic venture would result in anything resembling long-term success.

Nor had we even begun to grasp at that juncture the ferocity of the battles for survival to come—or the emotional and even physical toll they would exact.

But if we had known, would it have made a difference?

Probably not.

Because what we were after was even more important to us than all that would come with financial success. It was complete independence, on our own terms.

Don't get us wrong—the fact that a refurbished truck would end up launching a billion-dollar company was a very nice bonus.

One misconception that many who know us just from our (now multiple) appearances on *Shark Tank* seem to have: that the two of us are very similar people. In fact, in almost every respect—background and temperament, in our fundamental attitudes and assumptions—we could hardly be more different.

This is why we've decided to do this book as we have: with the two of us narrating in alternating sections, each giving his take on the events from his own perspective, in his own voice. Usually our versions more or less coincide, but not always. (And for additional perspective—and to keep us honest—we also occasionally include the voices/views of other key players in our story.)

Yes, we're cousins, it's right there on our trucks—but on closer examination, even that's only a *sort-of* situation.

One of us grew up in a secure and happy family, the other . . . well, let's just say it was different. One of us is so studiously scrupulous in his every choice he might as well be a member of the risk-averse Depression-era generation, for whom devastation lurked around every corner; the other long ago embraced a life philosophy of *Fuck it.*

Ultimately this is the very heart of our story. How we might've come apart, but didn't; how at the worst of it we hung together as people and as partners, along the way finding others who shared our vision and our values to build a team that's been more and more like a family.

If that sounds soft and sentimental, it's not—it makes both human and hard-nosed business sense.

There are whole books on staffing and personnel they make business-school students read, most of them as boring as their covers.

Think of this as telling how it works in real life.

We think it's pretty entertaining, in parts even funny.

Trust us, much of it was not at the time.

CHAPTER 1

Bloody Noses

JIM

A few days before we were to tape our first appearance on *Shark Tank*, Sabin and I were on the phone with the show's producers, doing prep, when one of them asked: "So how, exactly, are you guys related?"

We're on speakerphone, and my mom and dad and sister are also in the room, so I mute the phone and go, "Oh shit, how *are* we related?"—and they all crack up. Because it's a family joke that from a very young age I could never nail down the family tree.

So I just start riffing. "Well, actually I guess we're second cousins, because Sabin's mother is Jeannie Lomac, which is also the maiden name of my mom, Julie, so they're first cousins. So it's Jeannie, Julie, and our other aunt, Aunt Lynee, and they were the women who ran the show when it came to parties and gatherings, 'cause it sure as hell wasn't my dad. Anyway, they all grew up in Maine, really close to one another."

Meanwhile, Sabin's shooting me this look, older cousin to younger cousin, which says *Shut the hell up, don't screw this thing up!*

But it's not like I can stop now. I tell her about how our family extends from Cape Elizabeth to Scarborough to Biddeford, though Sabin's grandparents also lived in San Diego for his grandfather's military career.

I babbled on so long I'm sure she was sorry she'd asked. But in addition to kind of dodging the question, what I wanted to convey was how unique Maine is. How it's so small that it's like everyone is connected to everyone else. I mean, in my town, Cape Elizabeth, we had no streetlights, no fast food, and I literally knew every single person in my high school. And since I was a hockey player, I knew guys in high schools across the entire state.

Which was part of what we'd be pitching on the show—not just ourselves and our business, or even lobster, but the Maine experience. Because this wasn't some impersonal venture. Between Sabin and me, we'd grown up with at least twenty guys who are now lobstermen. Not all of them went to college, they stayed in Maine, and it's a good bet their kids'll also stay and grow up to be lobstermen.

And it was important that the producers and show's viewers understand this is a wonderful, deeply honorable thing, and that beyond dollars and cents, this is what this company we'd started was all about.

In fact, a few days later, when we tape our episode, Mr. Wonderful literally asks why he even needs us. Why can't he just do it himself, "throw millions of dollars at these guys and just buy whatever I need." Well, no, he can't, because these are generational businesses, from grandfather, to father, to the guys our age now, and it's rooted in a place where longtime relationships, and *trust*, matter.

And it's a good bet that those lobstermen he wants to buy off had an experience, maybe ten years ago, maybe fifty, where some rich guy waved the money at them, and they put up the lobster meat, and all of a sudden the money wasn't there or the buyer disappeared, or maybe he bought a lot the first time, but then he wasn't there the next year or the next quarter. And you can't run a wild-caught live-animal business that way. It really is largely a matter of doing business on handshakes and with people you know and trust.

But I'm getting *way* ahead of myself.

Sabin and I occupied a special place in the family dynamic—the only boys in our generation among a bunch of girls. Of course, he's three and a half years older, which to a kid can seem like a decade, and that gap only gradually closed as we grew older.

But the far bigger difference between us was in our life circumstances. That was huge. Sabe likes to say I came from the rich side of the tracks, and he was on the other side of the tracks, separating me in Cape Elizabeth from him in Scarborough. But the real difference was that I had stability and security in my life, and he never did. I had a mom and dad, and he was raised by a single mother. We had enough money, and he didn't. He was always at risk of falling off the rails. Sabe was constantly in and out of trouble. I could hardly even imagine that kind of existence.

So within the family, Sabin was always the bad boy, and I was always the good boy.

And it's true, I definitely *was* a Goody Two-Shoes. My mom was a school nurse, literally in the same elementary school, middle school, and high school as I was, so I wasn't going to do anything bad even if I wanted to. But I *didn't* want to. What I wanted was to do right by my parents.

It's not like they insisted on it—my older sister Annie certainly wasn't perfect—it was just my mindset. That's how my brain is wired to this day. I've always been someone who cares deeply about doing things right. At school, I always wanted to do really well, to get A's on tests, and if I didn't, I'd be pissed off and want to study more. I wasn't a nerd; I just wanted to make sure I was prepared and fully organized, leaving as little as possible to chance.

Who knows, probably some of it was innate. But of course it also had to do with what I saw every day. I'd watch my mom clean and vacuum the house and do the dishes before she went to work, and be totally there for us when she came home. I watched my father work from eight to five as the CFO at Goodwill Industries of Northern New England—and as soon as he got home he'd start mowing the lawn or cutting back the hedges, or chopping wood, or doing whatever else had to be done. There was never even a passing thought of paying a gardener or a landscape company or anyone else for something he could do himself.

I mean, these were people who *lived* their values, and they do to this day.

When I was twelve, my dad found out that his church—he's Greek Orthodox—was looking for a commercial cleaner to clean the building after Sunday services. He saw it as an opportunity. "Jim," he said, "how'd you like to help clean the church with me?"

It was not intended as a question. So for the next seven years of my life, until I went to college, every Sunday after church I spent three or four hours cleaning the church toilets and pews, vacuuming and mopping the floors.

It paid thirty bucks or so, which certainly came in handy, since if I wanted something beyond necessities, I had to earn the money to pay for it. But the real opportunity was to watch the quiet humility of this fifty-year-old man working alongside me, bleaching the toilets of the people that he'd just gone to church with.

That didn't change even after I started rising up the ranks in hockey. My father would drive me all over New England and Canada for tournaments, from Thursday through the weekend, and when we got home on Sunday, exhausted and sweaty and gross after playing six games, and when all the other kids were getting to shower and have dinner on the couch, I was still going with him to church to vacuum and clean.

It shaped my whole sense of everything. Definitely my sense of money. It was a pivotal thing in my life.

Sabin didn't have anything close to that in *his* life. At that age he was getting into all kinds of trouble, things I heard about when listening to my mom and dad talk in the other room.

But here's the thing. Once I got older, and the age gap seemed less important, when we got together as a family for a pool party or a holiday, the two of us would have a blast. When we'd get sick of the girls, which was pretty quickly, we'd ditch them and hang out.

We were both athletes, super competitive. He was more basketball and soccer; I was more hockey and lacrosse. So if we're playing basketball, he's gonna dominate me, and if we play street hockey, I dominate him. But either way, it could get pretty rough. I mean, the guy would fucking elbow you in the face without a second thought, and sometimes my nose would start bleeding like a sonovabitch.

But I gave as good as I got, and no one ever went crying to his mom. And after that we'd usually go upstairs and play NHL '94 on Super Nintendo. Sabe was always the Chicago Blackhawks. I was always the Boston Bruins, and we'd do it right, making like the PA announcer: "*Starting at forward, number 8, Cam Neely . . . in goal for Boston, number 35, Andy Moog.*" Since in '94 the actual Blackhawks had Ed Belfour in goal, who in real life later became an alcoholic, we'd usually build that into the action, like: "Uh-oh, Ed's drunk, he's drifted into the corner, he can't make the save!"

So when we were hanging out, it was all good. We never really talked much about the rest of our lives.

By the way, a lot of my strongest memories of those family get-togethers involved lobster. Both our mothers, my mom, Julie, and Sabe's mom, Jeannie, were total lobster fanatics. They couldn't get enough of it. No matter the occasion, even if it was Christmas or Thanksgiving, there'd always be lobster, along with the ham or turkey. They'd have a glass of Chardonnay in one hand, and just tear into these steamed lobsters with the other, picking out the meat, slathering it in butter, squeezing a lemon on top, just devouring them. Afterward, it would look like something some crazed scavenger left behind at the beach, just random bits of shell.

Who knows, subliminally it might've had an effect on the two of us.

It's not as if all that many people in Maine thought of lobster that way. I mean, it was pretty much a commonplace grocery item, you could go to any local food store, and they'd have a bunch of fresh lobster.

When I worked on tour boats back in high school, I used to tell tourists a local fable about how Maine state prisoners once rioted because they got so sick of getting served lobster six out of seven nights a week, and the only reason it wasn't served on the seventh night is that it was considered cruel and unusual punishment. It always got a big laugh. But, I swear, my mom probably would've found a way to end up in prison if she knew that was going to be the punishment, and her only issue would be *not* getting it on Sundays.

The fact is, I had to leave Maine to really understand what lobster meant to people living in other places. I went to college not all that far away, at Holy Cross in Worcester, Massachusetts, because I played hockey. Early on I had buddies from Canada and Alaska I brought home to Cape Elizabeth for a weekend, and they were like: *Holy shit, this is where you live? In this beautiful quaint little town, with no fast food and no streetlights, and gorgeous beaches, and all the lobster you can eat?*

So after that, when my buddies came up, I'd do the whole dog and pony show, and I'd take them to one of the little seafood shacks that looked like they were about to fall over but served tuna or halibut right off the boat; or maybe we'd just buy a bunch of fresh lobsters and bring 'em home, and my parents would steam them up out back, and, again, they'd be like: *Holy shit, this is what you guys eat?*

Well, that's not something you forget, and it certainly changed my perspective on things, and of course it all came back full circle when Sabin and I started the business.

But it probably never would have happened if it hadn't been for those bloody noses in the street, and the Nintendo games afterward.

In fact, when we first launched Cousins Maine Lobster and I moved to California, I brought out my Super Nintendo. And over all the time since then, whenever we've needed to clear our heads—whether because things were going well and there were new opportunities we had to evaluate, or because they were going to shit, and we thought, *Damn, we started on* Shark Tank, *and it looks like we might end up on* Dateline NBC—we'd pull it out and play a few games. And Moog's still making unbelievable saves for the Bruins, and Belfour's still staggering around on the ice for the Blackhawks.

Does it answer our questions or solve our problems? Hell, no. But it really works. It gets our minds right. No matter what else is happening, we're transported to those long-past days back in Maine.

SABIN

Soon after Barbara Corcoran became our business partner, she told me something that still resonates with me in an incredibly personal way. She said that she only invests in entrepreneurs who've had serious hardships in their lives, because she's seen how it fuels them.

Man, was that me.

The defining fact of my life is growing up without a father. I know that gets said so often, by so many people, that it's almost a cliché. It hardly even registers. To really grasp it, you actually have to have spent your childhood living it.

From an early age, I knew my life wasn't ideal. My dad was never present, my mom struggled a lot with her own issues, we didn't have a lot of money, and I felt alone . . . a lot. Without any brothers and sisters and living in a remote part of town, my home life was not amazing. My mother was raised by a tough Marine father, which I think really had a profound effect on her. Alcoholism ran in our family, and it was a constant presence within our household, among other issues. I struggle, now, with how to properly phrase these feelings, but I trust that anyone who has been through such struggles can understand what I am describing.

Through a lot of therapy, I realized I went into survival mode at a very young age and really have just begun winding down that fight-or-flight mode. I remember getting into trouble when I was a kid and telling myself that I had all the excuses to do so, and that no one could be mad at me for those decisions. But that sucked, and I wanted nice things and a nice life. So I decided early on, I mean *consciously decided*, that no way was I going to let this reality define me for the rest of my life.

I can remember the very night I made that decision. I was fourteen years old, in jail, and I thought, *Man, this just* isn't *the life I want. Okay, I've got all the excuses—no dad, no money, a mom with problems of her own. So here I am, and it sucks. 'Cause all I want is to have a family, and have money, and be able to do cool things, and it's not happening.*

But at that moment I knew with absolute certainty that it would. I would *make* it happen. I would control all the elements in my life that were controllable, and no matter what I did, no one would ever outwork, outthink, or outhustle me.

The fact is, though I'd only recognize this later, by then I'd already had one key piece of luck. I was born in San Diego, but at the age of four, we left. One morning, my mom loaded me and whatever else she could fit in our two-door Honda Prelude and took off for Maine. We drove for sixish days and I was clueless as to where we would end up. In the end, Maine was our new home and one that would have a profound impact on my life.

So as hard as my life was, at least I had a chance. Because if I'd stayed in San Diego, there's no doubt I would have found many more ways to slip through the cracks. Maine was a much more simple and easy life with fewer distractions. There was trouble, but you really had to work hard to find it.

Our family were Mainers from way back, so though my mom hadn't lived there for a long time, she was essentially heading home. She was born in Maine, and so were her parents. Her father was a thirty-year Marine colonel. They'd moved around a lot, and he ended up retiring in San Diego. So that's where my mom went to college, and it's where she had me. My parents never married; they just had a little fling. As soon as my dad found out mom was pregnant, he took off.

My mom was a hippie—the pot, the clothes, the beads, all of it—and came from one of those families that split over the war. Her dad was this tough old military guy, incredibly hard-headed, and she was out in the streets screaming "Fuck Vietnam." I ended up being very close with my grandfather, but he was as stubborn as they come—a quality I inherited. To illustrate this: While my mom's senior prom photos were being taken in their backyard, my grandfather came home buzzed up and threw the guy in the pool, tux and all. In other words: My mom wanted a clean break from everyone and everything San Diego, and she knew that Maine was the best bet for raising me.

I'm sure that was part of why she left. That, and because she had extended family back in Maine. But she also hoped I might somehow develop a relationship with my father, who was an Italian guy from the north end of Boston, only about an hour and a half away from southern Maine.

And to some extent that happened. I met him when I was around five and for a while would see him every few months. But by now he had another family, and our visits were very few and far between. What I mainly remember is not wanting to see him, and that it was uncomfortable and I didn't like it. I was probably ten when I stopped seeing him, and I didn't see him again until I was maybe forty. The only reason I did then was that I felt maybe I was punishing my own son by not letting him know his grandfather. So I allowed them to meet.

At first the guy acted like he was really appreciative. But after about a year and a half of being more present, he disappeared again. I don't know, it could be he stayed around even that long because he'd seen me on TV, and he figured I was making a lot of money. Whatever, at that point I wanted nothing more to do with him, and I told him to never contact our family again. He's not a man, that's all I can say. A man would never do that to a kid.

So let's leave it there, because there's really nothing more about him that needs saying.

Anyway, when my mom and I arrived in Maine, we stayed with family for a little while. Then my mom found a vacation rental, right on the water, which was vacant because it was wintertime. It was in the town of Scarborough in an area called Pine Point. When the summertime came, we had to move out, and we ended up moving to a little house with no heat, a few blocks away. My mom had to put parachutes under the ceilings to catch the plaster, otherwise it would fall and hit you in the face while you slept. The house was always freezing cold, and I remember my mom telling me to put more layers on. In hindsight, it was wild. But this was the mid-eighties and this was our life.

My mom was a lot more out of place in Maine than in California. Our license plate read "BE LOVE," which I'm sure baffled most Mainers, and of course she grew pot in the house. There was never a time in my life when I wasn't around weed.

But my mom always worked. She'd been to college and was a speech therapist. In fact, she worked in both my middle school and high school. It wasn't like Jim's situation with his mom, though—keeping an eye on me was not in her parenting wheelhouse. True to her hippie origins, she basically encouraged me to do whatever the hell I wanted, and to live my life on my own terms. Which, given that I was a pretty wild kid, may not have been the best advice.

On the other hand, it definitely fostered independence and the idea there were no limits. I could tell her, "Hey, I'm gonna be an astronaut" or whatever the hell else crossed my mind, and her attitude would be "Go for it."

And that ended up being a priceless gift. Even if it was inadvertently or irresponsibly given, I'll always be grateful for it. Mom, if you're reading this, thank you. This was the best parenting decision you ever made.

For instance, at twelve or thirteen I became intrigued with New York, and she had no problem letting me take the bus from Maine to Manhattan and stay in youth hostels. I did it multiple times.

As I mentioned, my mom had a lot of family in the area—cousins and second cousins, some of whom were like brothers and sisters—and of course they were a lot more responsible. I always loved family get-togethers because they gave me time with my cousins and allowed me a sense of normalcy. I hated when the holidays would end.

So it was me and her—no sisters or brothers, not even many other kids in the neighborhood. And I could get to feeling pretty isolated, especially since my mom had plenty of demons of her own. And she made some really bad choices involving men. For a while she dated this guy with a hook for a hand. I swear, he'd come to the house looking like a pirate, and it would scare the living shit out of me. Another guy she married for maybe one year, and then he was gone. I mean, she had her own shit to deal with, her own challenges. And there were times, lots of them, that I was a pretty pissed-off kid.

But here's the thing: I almost never showed it. In fact, what people mainly saw was the opposite—this upbeat, fun-loving kid who was the life of every party. And, weird as it may sound, that part was real, too, because alienated as I was, I was also incredibly social by nature. I was funny, I was good-looking, and I was a *great* athlete. And, especially in high school, that went a long way.

I loved making people happy, and making them laugh and feel good was my specialty. I still possess these traits today, and if you ask anyone who knows me, they would say these characteristics are extremely apparent. I suppose I was giving people what I always wanted and needed back, what I lacked growing up.

School, for me, was amazing. I actually loved going to school, because that's where the action was—sports, girls, *life*. I was social and popular, and it was a great opportunity for me to talk to the prettiest girls and get their phone numbers. All right, maybe I wasn't the greatest boyfriend material, but what can I say—I liked them all and could never settle. I'd stay that way for a long time.

As a freshman, I made varsity in soccer. By sophomore year I was varsity basketball and baseball too. At the same time, I was the only kid whose father was never on the sidelines, and the one for whom the coaches had to buy cleats and basketball shoes. I never said a word about it, but it's hard to describe how much those things ate at me. I remember those great coaches who bought me things we couldn't afford, the soccer cleats or shin pads; I vividly remember those interactions to this day. That's why I mentor kids and try my best to give back. I know what it feels like to be in that position, and it breaks my heart to see people struggling.

Sports were everything to me as a kid. I wish I had given them more of my time and passion, but I was distracted. If I'd focused, there's no doubt I'd have gone on to play soccer or basketball at a higher level. In fact, even though back then there was very little recruiting in Maine, I did have a couple of scholarship offers. But I turned them down. Why? Probably because I had no one telling me not to, and I just wanted to move to New York City to party.

Sports were also a great outlet for my aggression—I loved fighting as much as playing. I was never the biggest kid out there, but I felt I had the biggest heart and I was very, very aggressive. I wanted to crush everyone standing in the way of our team's success. I wasn't kind; I was there to win at all costs. That fire, in hindsight, was likely due to my own inner anger and displeasure with my home life. But in the moment, all I knew was that if someone wanted a fight, they didn't need to look any further than me.

I was never a bully, *ever*. To the contrary, I was always kind to people—and to the underdog kids especially. In fact, one of my great pleasures was beating the crap out of bullies.

The soundtrack of my life was rap music. I got infatuated with it when I was twelve or thirteen, and even now, a lot of it is etched on my brain. These artists were talking about things I totally related to—single-parent families, scraping by on a low income—and with an attitude I totally respected: If you didn't let those things destroy you, they made you stronger and tougher.

It's the reason I started taking those trips down to New York, to get music you couldn't find in Maine. I'd get to the bus terminal and immediately head down to Canal Street in Chinatown to load up on tapes. While I was there I'd also pick up the clothes you couldn't find in Maine. I was fascinated by New York, the culture, the nightlife, the *action*; it felt like where I belonged.

My mom, meanwhile, was drinking heavily, so things weren't exactly stable at home. Our lives were even more unsettled than usual; I didn't hesitate to give her a lot of shit, and things could get pretty heated between us. One time, in a rage, she actually clocked me with a frying pan. What set her off was that I'd taken a needle and inked myself a tattoo, a little cross on my arm. Still there, and in my opinion still looks fine—maybe not professional, but a decent jailbird job. But she didn't agree.

Things got so bad that for a while I went to live with my aunt Lynne and my uncle Andrew. They were a very different kind of family—normal. They were kind to one another, and there was always good food in the fridge. To this day, I am still very close with them and have so much appreciation for the love they gave me as a child. They always showed up for me. Thank you, guys.

Jimmy's family was the same way, another good example of what a nice, normal family could be. I didn't see them quite as often, mainly just at big family get-togethers, but since Jim and I were the only boys among a bunch of girls, we always had a bit of a bond. Still, with the age difference, it was a while before we got really close.

From early on, Jim was very involved in hockey, and he was seriously talented. But what really struck me was seeing him with his dad, who would drive him to the ends of the earth to support his hockey career. He pushed him and supported him, and he did all the things he needed to do so Jimmy'd reach his potential. And Jimmy should've played in the NHL; he was that good—tough and quick and unbelievably strong.

Anyway, I eventually ended up back home with my mom, and soon things would be bad again. Until finally I basically just said to myself: *Fuck it, I'm so strong I don't need anyone else, nothing will ever hurt me, blah blah blah.* In my own mind, I went overnight from being a kid to being an adult, truly becoming the man of the house. I remember my grandfather telling me (at the age of thirteen) that I was the man of the house and I needed to behave like one. I interpreted that to mean: Buckle up, toughen up, be strong.

The first time I got busted for something I was thirteen or fourteen, and it was for the stupidest goddamn thing ever. A bunch of us had gotten tickets for a Puff Daddy (as he used to be known) concert down in Worcester, Massachusetts, and on the day of the show there was a massive snowstorm. My mom of course had no trouble with my going anyway, but most of the other kids' parents put their feet down and kept them home, so a few friends and I were stuck with all these unused tickets. We figured we'd sell those tickets when we got there. So we drove through this blizzard, and when we got to the venue, we started trying to sell the extra tickets, and almost immediately one of my friends sold a pair to an undercover cop.

The cops surrounded us, demanding we hand over the rest of the tickets—which I was holding. And I thought: *We just drove three hours through a blizzard, they aren't getting our tickets,* and so I turned and took off. But I slipped on the ice, and I got into a scuffle with the cops. They threw me in jail—not juvey, Big Boy jail. They stripped me, searching for weapons, and even looked up my ass (something I remember vividly, yikes). It was pretty scary.

Although this might've been my "scared straight" moment, it wasn't. I flirted with trouble, police, and authority in general a lot more throughout my teenage years. For me, this defined me and made me feel tougher. In hindsight, I'm sad for my younger self and sad for such ignorance. I'm also sad for the people I hurt along the way, but that's a part of life, I guess.

Through all of this, believe it or not, I pretty much kept up my grades, at least as much as I cared to. I got A's and B's, the occasional C; but I was smart enough to have been a straight-A student if I'd given a shit. In fact, when I chose to use it, I had the ability to achieve almost any goal I set my mind to. For instance, one thing I *did* care about, passionately, was fairness and equal opportunity. So I ran for student council and started a civil rights group in high school.

I realize it sounds pretty schizophrenic, because it was. On one hand, a star athlete and all-around good kid, on the other, this angry kid who was constantly looking for trouble.

Looking back, I can only say that every step of the way I was watching and listening and picking up lessons that would come in very handy.

As rough as those years were, and often painful, they left me with a mix of qualities that pushed me to get ahead on my own terms: a determination to not just work as hard as it takes, but have a blast doing it; to power on in the face of adversity; to never shy away from risk.

Crucially, those times sharpened my instincts about people. Even now, walking into a room for a social gathering or a business meeting, in two minutes I can have everyone relaxed and laughing—but even as I'm doing it, in my head I'll be sussing out who's for real and who's full of shit.

JIM

Do the Basics

I'm a fierce competitor. I don't just want to beat the other guy, what I want is . . . how to put this delicately? I want to dominate, to win, and always come out ahead of competitors.

Even today, that's a huge part of the way I define myself in business.

I may have been born with this instinct, but it was honed over my early years as a hockey player.

Growing up in Maine, you either played hockey or you skied; it was axiomatic. But in my case, for a long time I did neither. While most of my friends were skating when they were four or five, and into organized hockey by seven or eight, I basically watched from the sidelines. It wasn't until I was almost ten when my dad suggested—in that way of his that meant it was more than just a suggestion—that it might be time for me to lace up a pair of skates. And I actually had a crying fit.

It probably only took my dad that long because he himself had been the rare Maine kid who'd never played hockey. Growing up in a fatherless home, they hadn't had money for the equipment. So even now, he hardly knew any more about what to do than I did. There's a photo of me in front of our house the first time he dressed me to go skate, and my shin pads are outside of my socks, instead of tucked hidden underneath. My buddies, who'd been whizzing around the ice for years, stick handling the puck, thought it was the funniest thing they'd ever seen. And I felt as ridiculous as I looked.

But soon enough I began to catch up and then some. In fact, within a year I knew this was something I wanted to do seriously. I just got that buzz, and I wanted more, and I wanted to do it really well.

Being the way I am, I went after it. By twelve, I was going to the gym five or six days a week after school, and afterward to the track to do plyometrics and run sprints to make my legs stronger and my reflexes faster and build that physical foundation.

Most everyone's got a dream, and mine couldn't have been clearer: I was going to play hockey, I'd play Division 1 in college and then, if things broke right, I'd go pro. It's not like I was delusional. I realized the percentage of people who got to do that is very, very small. Still, I was focused in a way not very many people that age were. That was my goal, and it was front and center. Every night, when homework was done, I'd go out to the driveway with a big bucket of pucks, put on a pair of Rollerblades, lay down a plexiglass surface on the driveway, and practice shooting on net. If it was summertime, and there was still some sun out, great. If not, I'd turn on the garage lights and keep shooting.

Already, probably from watching my dad, I understood the ways to success. Put in the work. Stay focused. Do things that other people won't. Always be looking to take the next step up. All pretty basic. But it's amazing how many people blow off the basics.

Between the work in the gym and the practice in the driveway, as well as competing in local leagues, within a couple of years I'd overtaken my buddies. And by the time I was sixteen, playing with guys two or three years older on our high school team, I was not only the best player on that team but among the best in my age group in the entire state.

This became clear when I tried out for one of the select teams that a couple of years before would have seemed an impossible reach. Called Team New England, it was to be composed of players from all the New England states, so there were hundreds of kids trying out. The talent level was way beyond anything I'd experienced, including guys who were a cinch to be top Division 1 players.

Seeing this, at first I'm like, *Shit, no way can I compete against these guys!!!* I mean, I'm looking out on the ice and there's Greg Moore, this big-bodied kid out of Auburn, Maine, who played for Saint Dominic's, whom up to now I've only read about. He'll go on to play at the University of Maine and then become a top-10 draft pick in the NHL's first round. So I'm super intimidated, and have no expectations, and neither does my dad. But I go out and make the team, and Greg Moore becomes my buddy, along with four or five other guys who'll later be NHL draft picks.

So Team New England goes to St. Paul, Minnesota, for a tournament against teams from other regions—the West Coast, the Pacific

Northwest, the Southeast, Mid-Atlantic—ten teams in all, comprised of all the best players born in 1984. With twelve forwards per team times ten, that made 120 forwards in all, and out of that group, I get ranked twenty-ninth, based on pro and Division 1 potential.

But while that was somewhat encouraging, it also made it clear how steep a climb remained. In fact, during the tournament, more than one D1 college coach told my father that if I was going to play college hockey at the highest level, I'd better leave Maine, because the competition level there just wasn't what it needed to be.

And that made sense to me. I knew that to take the next step up, I needed to be around other players with my kind of drive and desire, and where there'd be more eyes on me from scouts.

But it also seemed like a good idea because I could see what was happening to a lot of the kids at my school in Cape Elizabeth, including some of my teammates. As a freshman and sophomore, it was obvious to me that the older guys, and even some my age, were heading for a fall. We'd come home on the bus from an away game, and the only thing on their minds was to run out and party. I didn't drink at all until I was seventeen or eighteen, and even then I'd only maybe have an occasional beer. You'd sure as hell never find me out in the woods after school, smoking weed. But some people I knew were out there all the time, including some hockey players with a ton of potential. They were caught up in a social life that had nothing to do with maximizing their talent, and they were going to fall off the map.

So in hockey terms, I always knew it was a process of attrition. There were some very talented kids who were out there doing this shit every day, going into the woods behind the track to rip a joint during lunch break or in between classes, and I recall thinking how they would likely be hurting their chances in the hockey space.

I mean, I could see this with 100% certainty. The one time I did go out into the woods, I'd see all these guys that I played hockey with, and they and the girls were so stoned you couldn't communicate with them. I was like, *What the fuck is everyone doing? Why get distracted from what you're trying to do, even if it's just to use hockey to get a good education?*

I know they didn't exactly appreciate my attitude, either—they thought I was a pussy. But I really just didn't get why they'd do it to themselves. It's not that I thought it made them bad people, and it didn't mean they wouldn't grow up to have great lives. It just took them out of the game.

So I left my hometown at seventeen to go to boarding school at Phillips Exeter Academy in New Hampshire. I played my junior and senior years there, and it definitely was a step up in competition.

During my senior year, I was recruited to Boston University, the University of Vermont, and Colorado College, which at the time was the number one hockey program in the country. But since the offers didn't come with scholarship money, I decided to do a year of junior hockey before committing to a school.

And that's where things started to go south.

Given hockey's speed and sheer physicality, even those who play marvel that anyone ever makes it through relatively intact. I wouldn't be one of the lucky ones. Over the course of my fairly brief career, I had four major concussions.

The one I had that year in junior hockey was the worst. I got hit from behind and went headfirst into the boards—not the glass, but effectively into a cement wall. I ended up missing twenty-five games of a sixty-game schedule.

Still, at the time, it didn't feel like anything more than a temporary setback. In fact, my first game back a bunch of D1 schools were in the stands.

Except what they saw was a totally different player. I was skating over pucks as if they weren't there, not even touching them. I remember my coach saying, "Well, you're just going to have to get back to some of the basics." After being gone so long, that process took a while.

What I probably should have done at that point was take a long break before coming back, and then probably aimed for Boston College or Harvard. Those were always my dream schools, and, though I might not have been a full scholarship guy, between a full recovery and my previous record, I probably could have gotten in and then seen how it went.

But that's not what I did. I instead went to Holy Cross, and I had a very mediocre-at-best end to my career. My coach and I never saw eye to eye, and for the first time ever I was a fourth-line guy. So, hockeywise, it was a really, really bad last four years, a total shitstorm and mind fuck to boot. I mean, my parents would come to a game and half the time I wouldn't even play.

It really wore on me. Growing up I'd had all kinds of coaches: Some were really kind and some were dicks; some were friendly with the team and others would be assholes and skate you harder. No problem with any of that. But this guy was different; he was dishonest and devastated me on an emotional level.

For me it was hell, not to mention an incredible comedown after making Team New England at sixteen, getting recruited to go to Exeter, and having various schools trying to entice me. The fact is, it would have been really easy to be like, *I'm outta here*, and transfer to a Division 3, or just quit playing entirely.

But at the same time, there was tremendous camaraderie with my teammates. Some had had experiences similar to mine, others different, but fifteen years later, eight guys from that group are my closest friends. So there was the contrast between these friendships I'd never have made if I didn't go there—and the sporting side where everything sucked.

No exaggeration, those were the toughest four years of my life. But I'll never forget what my dad said to me when I came out on the other side, telling me how proud he was of me for having put up with it and not let it break me. For all my achievements, he'd never said anything like that before. And what I realize now is that it was full circle for him also, from that first day when he had no idea how to dress me, all the way through the long period of adversity and emotional turmoil. It was as if, together, we'd accomplished what as a parent he'd set out to do.

CHAPTER 2

Hustling

YOUNGER VERSIONS

SABIN

I've always had a great work ethic; that was never a problem. Even from a very young age, I was out there hustling. I don't know any other way.

My first job was at a place called The Clambake, just a couple of blocks down from the house I live in today, washing dishes and making coleslaw. At other places I was a waiter or a busboy. I delivered pizzas at Pizza Time and was a line cook at Chili's. I did food prep at a place called Lois's Natural, and I served breakfast at another called the Sand Dollar Inn. Then, too, I worked for a while at a window tinting place and also did a stint at Best Buy. I mean, I probably had thirty-plus local jobs in my small town of Scarborough, Maine.

And then there's one that, for a kid from my background, nobody would ever predict.

When I was ten or eleven, I started acting.

It was my mom who got me into it. Back in San Diego she'd been an actor—she appeared in some legit stuff at the Old Globe theater, the major house out there—and she got me involved with a little talent agency in our town. They set me up to do local jobs—print or commercials for businesses in the area. I did one for a local arcade called The Dream Machine, and another for a sandwich shop called Amato's and a bunch of other small, local commercials.

Those experiences whetted my appetite for the big time—which was pretty much anywhere outside Maine, but especially New York, since by then I'd already started going there as often as I could, anyway.

And, again, my mom stepped up. I can't remember the exact sequence, but she'd been sending out head shots, and lo and behold, I was signed by a major New York modeling and talent agency. Soon I was doing some pretty high-profile stuff, and making decent money at it. I did print ads for Calvin Klein, Polo Ralph Lauren, and *The*

Wall Street Journal, and also some runway modeling, including a show by Versace.

By the time I graduate high school, I can't get out of Maine quick enough. Which doesn't mean I'm still not confused about my future. I can't decide whether I should continue on the entertainment/modeling path or pursue my other passion, social justice, and go into civil rights law.

So, kind of trying to have it both ways, I apply only to New York–based colleges: NYU, Marymount Manhattan, Manhattan University, Hofstra. I get into most of them, but I couldn't afford NYU. I visited Hofstra and I loved it. Close to NYC, a campus with tons to do, parties, life, the whole thing.

And that's how it went. At eighteen, I'm going to school full-time—taking a lot of classes on civil rights and acting—but running into Manhattan for modeling and acting auditions. I'm also doing a lot of acting at Hofstra; for four years I get the lead in every play, even as I'm sometimes also doing plays Off Broadway and getting parts in soaps like *All My Children* and *Guiding Light*. Nights I still loved to go out and party. I also worked full-time throughout my four years at Hofstra. I was a waiter at Morton's, providing me an opportunity to make tons of money.

I know it sounds like a lot, and it was, but I swear, it didn't feel that way. In fact, it sometimes felt like I wasn't as super focused as I should've been. Because by nature I'm just very, very ambitious, and shooting for the moon. I've never been someone who celebrates a supposed success or accomplishment for more than twenty minutes, because in my head I'm always on to the next thing. Like *Okay, that was good, but now what?* Because I always want more.

And what by then I wanted, specifically—I'm now really clear on this—was to make it as an actor. Do important movies and quality TV. Modeling was fine, it was a nice ego stroke, but ultimately it was frivolous.

And not only did I want to make it, I wanted to be a star.

Which meant relocating to LA. I stayed in New York for a few years after college, then made the inevitable move west. I'd already done a couple of things out there, and it was where both my personal manager and my new agency, Innovative Artists, were based. There was no question, in my mind or theirs, that I had the talent; but, so what? A lot of people have the talent. As with almost everything else, it was a matter of perseverance, will, and maximizing opportunity.

Right after the move, I got a part in a play—not a big break, but all good.

The play was at night, so I had my days free. And rather than just sitting on my ass waiting for the phone to ring with word of another audition for a commercial or a line or two on some TV show, I decided to get my real estate license. I don't even know what for, it's not like I ever thought I'd use it. Anyway, I took a class and took the California real estate exam—which, since I was always horrible at tests, I proceeded to flunk three times. But I just kept doing it until I finally passed.

Meanwhile, I'm continuing to audition, and getting some small acting jobs, and starting to get noticed a little bit, but still having trouble making the rent. And then I get a call from an old friend of my mom's who lives in town, and she tells me she's referred me to some young guys who are doing some really cool shit in real estate. Do I want an interview?

"Sure, whatever." I tell her I'm pretty busy, but I've got some time during the day.

The guys she introduces me to are young, good-looking, sharp business guys, who are starting to do these things called "short sales." Even though I had no clue what it's all about, I become the first agent they hire. The timing couldn't be better—or worse, depending how you look at it—because this was before the housing market crash. So fast-forward a couple of years, they end up being the number one short sale company in California, and I'm their top agent, with a couple of hundred listings, as well as managing the other real estate agents. So from basically being broke when I moved to LA, by 2010 and 2011, in my late twenties, I'm making half a million dollars a year.

To me, I'm *killing* it, totally living the life. I'm single, with a really cool one-bedroom in West Hollywood, partying all the time and going on three-week vacations all over the world.

Meanwhile I also still had my other career going—only now I have a totally different attitude. Because now I don't have to run out to Van Nuys to read for some Colgate commercial for $2,000. I can only go after stuff I want, which is incredibly liberating.

And things aren't going badly on that end, either, since I'm starting to get approached with more interesting material. But it's still a grind. At one point, I have a bunch of callbacks for the part of Meadow's boyfriend on *The Sopranos.* I ultimately didn't get it, but I was pretty damn close. I was making progress, and I could feel it.

I wasn't one of those actors who said, *It's this or bust—I'm gonna do this 'til the day I die, and I will be broke and wait tables until it happens for me.* I mean, a lot of them are really convinced that one day someone's gonna see them in that Colgate ad and hire them for the lead in a big film, and they'll wake up and be a household name.

I wasn't that guy. I'd never bullshitted myself about anything before, and I wasn't about to start now. I'd been broke most of my life, and I hated it. I'd waited more than enough tables, and not having to do that anymore felt like the ultimate blessing. Maybe more than anything, I was sick of people I didn't like having control over me, and having to deal with their shit.

So as much as I liked acting and loved being creative, in the end I liked the idea of having my freedom and being solvent even more.

What's ironic—or maybe not, given the lunacy of the entertainment field—is that I had my greatest success in the business *after* I'd pretty much left it behind. Because after we opened Cousins, and it began taking off, I started getting calls from the Food Network. They thought I had "good energy," and asked me to be a guest judge on a couple of their shows, which led to my eventually hosting a couple of shows of my own.

My bosses in real estate are amazing; they become my true friends and they feel like family. The majority of them are Persian Jews, and being the only non-Jew in the friend group, they nickname me "the rabbi" when I attend every Friday's Shabbat dinner. The food and family feel was amazing. I longed for it and felt at peace when I was with them.

Not only were they smart and fun, they were very good at their job. They created an exceptional work culture, people actually looked forward to going to work there. It was mainly little, seemingly inconsequential things—everyone periodically going out together for drinks and a catered dinner, for instance—but what they were consciously creating was an atmosphere that was upbeat and welcoming and fostered a genuine sense of common purpose.

And that's something we would try to do when we started Cousins Maine Lobster—hiring people we actually liked being around, and doing our part to create a positive work culture—and it's proven absolutely vital to our success.

Would I have stayed in real estate very much longer? Might it ultimately have been my career? Hard to say. I liked a lot about it, starting with the friendships and very much including the money, not to mention the freedom it bought. Then again, I'm not built that way. I've got an entrepreneur's restless brain, so the question will probably always be: What's next?

Anyway, it soon became moot, because one day in February 2011, I picked up the phone and there was Cousin Jimmy. "Hey," he said, "I'm in LA, got time to get together?"

JIM

A Boston Winter

Looking back, if my college hockey career was one of the most miserable experiences of my life, it was also one of the best things that ever happened to me. Because having survived those four years of psychic torture and having come out intact, I had no doubt I could survive anything—or anyone—I had to.

And, sure as shit, the early years of Cousins Maine Lobster would put that to the test. Inexperienced and naïve as we were, the trials and tribulations were never ending, and there were times our running joke about starting on *Shark Tank* but ending up on *Court TV* or *Dateline* seemed less funny than prophetic. But every time there was a new setback, in the back of my mind there'd be a voice: *I did that, I can do this.*

I'd always been a realist; as an athlete, even before the injuries, I knew the odds were stacked against my making it to the pros. So if Plan A hit the rocks, I was never going to be adrift. Plan B was to have a strong academic background leading to a great professional career, whatever it ended up being.

And that's what I ultimately got from Holy Cross. Thinking I might like a career in law, by sophomore year I'd chosen political science as my major. But I was keeping my options open, doing a lot of networking with alums from both Holy Cross and Exeter to see what opportunities there might be out there.

This led to an internship in the summer after my junior year with Northwestern Mutual Insurance. I was sharing a place with a hockey buddy who had an internship at a medical device company. So we'd get together after work and compare notes. My stories were about making cold calls to people and trying to sell them insurance, his were about hanging out with doctors who explained the latest treatments for cardiovascular disease.

So what I found out that summer was (a) I loved sales, but (b) I'd love it a helluva lot more if I could be passionate about what I was selling.

I immediately started reaching out to anyone I knew who was either a doctor or knew one or, even better, had a connection to a medical device company. Eventually I set up a couple of interviews, one of which was with a company called Stryker Orthopaedics.

After going through several rounds of interviews with sales reps and the general manager, I wind up sitting with the two owners in their big corner office. They're in their sixties and clearly well to do—I've noticed the Mercedes in the parking lot—and right off the bat one of them tells me, "You know, it's a huge responsibility to work with doctors in the operating room, because that's what our sales reps have to do. Most people your age don't start their careers in this industry. They get here fifteen years down the line after they've sold wine or copiers or insurance."

His partner adds that, in fact, Stryker Orthopaedics has never hired anyone just out of college.

Now, I have zero sales experience, not counting the insurance cold calls, which I'm pretty sure isn't gonna help my case, and at this point I haven't even graduated from college. So I'm realizing this is going to be an even bigger lift than I expected.

"Well, then," I said, "let me be the first."

Because, hey, if I couldn't even sell myself, what good could I be to them?

I went on to explain that this was an opportunity not just for me but for them. I was hungrier and more motivated than anyone else and, yes, probably also a little cheaper. Though I had no experience in the field, going forward, no one was more worth putting the resources into. Then I got into my resume: This is what I achieved in hockey; here's all the Sundays I helped clean our church; look at my grades in college. I might be green, but nobody will put in more time and effort, and I'll learn what I need to know faster than anyone else. Yes, getting thrown straight into the fire might be at times rough, and I'll have to learn the hard way, but you won't ever be sorry you gave me the opportunity.

And of course the whole time I'm very conscious that this is a kind of audition, because as they listen to my pitch, what they're also hearing is how I would represent the company professionally to doctors, nurses, administrators, right through to the janitors.

And as I go on, I realize that these guys are seeing in me a little of their younger selves, when after a stint working in corporate America, they had the courage to strike out for themselves and start a Stryker distributor.

So, yes, I got the job. And by the time I left four years later to start Cousins Maine Lobster in 2012, they were hiring a lot of kids right out of college.

Meanwhile, the job turned out to be just as interesting as I'd hoped. We sold a variety of products used in orthopedic surgery—Stryker is a big player in total knees and total hips—but my role specialized in trauma products such as nails and plates. We had nails for everything: one to go into the femur for a femoral fracture, another for a hip fracture, others designed for the tibia or to go into the humerus. The same with plates: certain plates for broken ankles, and others for broken wrists or fractured elbows.

I did really well from the start. Why? Because my pitch hadn't been b.s. Not being fifty, and not having the experience, I *was* curious and eager to learn, and the doctors I was dealing with appreciated that. They knew I was for real, and though I obviously wanted to make the sale, that's not all I was about. Doctors have a reputation for being egotistical pricks and not having time for people like me, since they're saving people's lives. But with many of the doctors I met, my experience was the opposite.

I mean, I believed in our products; they were as good as or better than anything else on the market. But in the end a screw's a screw, right? So I was never pushy about our products. The fact is, I was genuinely fascinated by what I was seeing every day in hospitals, and over time I'd naturally develop a rapport with the people working there. I remember one teaching doctor telling me I asked more questions than his residents. But why wouldn't I? It was fascinating and I was engaged.

So the trust factor was huge. If I saw a rep from another company in a back hallway talking to a doctor who did 90% of his nails with me, I wouldn't be concerned, because I knew I was the one he wanted in his operating room.

Of course, that was the most interesting part of the job—and the most bizarre. I swear, if patients knew some of the stuff that goes on in operating rooms when they're under . . . I remember when I was first hired, one of the managers was like, *Dude, when you go home for Christmas, you're gonna be the talk of the Christmas parties. Everyone else'll be in finance or regular sales, and you'll be like, "I was in this operating room, and this guy crashed his motorcycle, and his leg was smashed up, and blood was coming from everywhere, and* **I** *had to tell the doctor the implementation protocol of our nails."*

We're not doctors or trained medical experts. However, we *were* experts in our products and their implementation. So when a doctor was cutting into someone's hip, and he turned to me and asked, "Hey, Jim, where am I making my insertion on my first drill point on this guy's hip?" it was my job to know, because I knew our product manual. So I'd go, "You're gonna make it on the one-third anterior and two-thirds posterior on the greater trochanter." That's where they'd put the drill and where they start drilling.

Now, I'm not doing the drilling, and I'm certainly not telling the doctor I know medicine like he does, but I am telling him the best chances for success with this product. So if they had to clean out a canal, drilling through it in order to put a nail down, you might advise them to start with a small drill, then go to a bigger drill, and then a bigger one, enlarging it very gradually to make sure the bone doesn't break; then I'd advise them where the screws should go based on product manuals.

Along the way, I experienced some remarkable things, and also some pretty sobering things. If it's eleven thirty at night, and someone comes into the ER with a broken hip, he might get a hand doctor doing the hip, because that's who happened to be on call, and he'd tell me, "Jeez, the last one of these I did was a year ago. I really need you, Jim." And I'm like, *Holy shit*, because this stuff's real. But the fact is,

I've seen four hundred hip fractures a year, and he hasn't, so I really am kind of a helpful mind.

Of course, I saw all kinds of stuff I wish I hadn't. I'd see doctors rushing through a procedure because they wanted to get home to their kids, and things being done I knew were incorrect—screws not all the way through or too far through, so they're gonna create pain or product failure. But then you'd also see some phenomenal outcomes, with doctors who cared deeply and took all the time necessary to see everything was exactly right.

I mean, it was a crazy, crazy, endlessly eye-opening job. And I loved it.

Meanwhile, I was living the life—young, unattached, making good money, and going to Bruins games with my buddies whenever I wanted.

So chances are excellent that if things had gone slightly differently I'd still be doing it. Except one of those freezing, depressing winter days in Boston—it's February 2011—I decide to take a quick trip to LA. Partly it's to see my old high school girlfriend and find out if there's still anything there and if we might get back together. But really it's to get out of the freakin' weather and because Sabin lives out there. I haven't seen him in forever. It's been so long, I don't even have his number, and have to ask my mom to get it from Aunt Jeannie.

But I don't tell my buddies that part. Saying I'm flying across the country to see this girl sounds exciting and romantic, and it's a lot less pathetic than, *Hey, I'm maybe gonna get to hang out with my cousin.*

CHAPTER 3

Extremely Under the Influence

WHEN WE HAD HAIR . . .

SABIN

"Hey," says Jimmy when he calls, "I'm here in LA for a few days! Want to get together?"

"Yeah, sure." But the truth is, I'm pretty busy around then, and just as inclined to blow him off. Anyway, he's with some girl he knew back east.

But then he texts a couple of days later. He says he's at lunch with the old girlfriend, but let's connect.

"Where exactly are you?" I text back. Because if you know LA, he could be five minutes away or more than an hour. And if, say, he's by the beach, no way am I about to drive all the way out there in the brutal late-afternoon traffic.

But he tells me he's at this restaurant in Beverly Hills—says it's in the same building as the William Morris Agency, next to an Equinox gym.

Holy shit! It's the same building as my real estate office, the one I'm in right now!

"Dude, I'm right above you, I'm coming down!"

I rush right downstairs, and there he is, with this girl, and immediately it's like, *Oh my God, what was I thinking, how could I imagine NOT seeing him?! This is awesome!*

Because though it's been years, nothing has changed. It's like we last talked yesterday.

Only he's with this girl, and I supposedly have to work, so they go off to do other stuff. But then, half an hour later, he calls me and suggests we hang out this evening.

I'm a very high energy guy to start with. Get me on a good day and you're in for some fun, and seeing Jimmy has lit a match under me. I decide I'm gonna give him the fucking night of his life.

And I sure as hell did.

The first place I take him to is this swanky sushi place on Sunset called Katana where there are always tons of celebrities, and even more hot girls. We sit outside on the terrace, catching up while we eat this fantastic sushi. And meanwhile we're drinking martinis, and tequila, and beer and wine, and getting absolutely hammered. But it's like old times, we're talking about everything—work and girls, and of course everything gets back to family.

My grandfather, my hero, had recently died, so he was really on my mind, and that led to his sister, who was Jimmy's grandmother. I told Jim how I took her to lunch whenever I was back in Maine—either bringing her Italian sandwiches or pizza, accompanied by her choice of either a caffeine-free Diet Coke or a beer. I loved just being with her and shooting the breeze. And I said how much I fucking hate it that so many people our age ignore their grandparents. Jim not only understood, but he felt the same way.

At some point we go across the street to a place called Skybar, but by now we're so far gone we get kicked out—very uncharacteristic of me, because I never get kicked out of places. And the next place we go, we get kicked out of there too. That's how totally, grossly drunk we were.

Still, the whole time we're talking. And eventually we get back on the subject of work. The fact is, before this I had no clue what he did for a living; for all I knew he could've been a salaried employee in a dentist's office. But as he tells me about it, I realize our jobs are pretty similar. Like me, he's working on commission, and doing great at it; like me he has the mentality of an entrepreneur.

I mean, the drunker we get, the more of a love fest it becomes. And finally I'm like, *Man, we should work together! Find something and just make it happen.*

So we start tossing around ideas, and at some point Jim says, "What about lobster?"

"What about it?"

"You know, why don't we do our own lobster place?"

And immediately we both recognize it's a great idea, because there's no place in Los Angeles that has lobster at all the way we remember it from growing up in Maine. And when we got into how it would work, we even hit on the idea of a food truck. I mean, we basically came up with the whole thing *extremely* under the influence.

So cut to the next morning in my one-bedroom apartment. I wake up and there's Jimmy, asleep on my air mattress. I go off to work, and by the time I get back that afternoon, he's gone, en route back to Boston.

So I assume that's it, right? Just a great night reconnecting with Jimmy.

It's like I'd forgotten how he was on the ice, that incredible tenacity.

JIM

"What's a Food Truck?"

When I arrived in California, Sabe and I had been out of touch for more than five years. I'd stuck close to home in New England; he'd gone off to school in New York and then moved out to LA for his acting career.

But when we see each other that afternoon, I mean *immediately*, we're right back where we were as kids, the same little cousin/big cousin dynamic, the same rapport, the same everything.

In theory, I've gone out to see the old girlfriend, and that's okay. But it isn't what it used to be, and no sense forcing it. Thanks but no thanks, and no ill will. In fact, a year later when we launch the truck, she'll work the register.

But Sabin, he's the perfect guy to rip around with in LA. He's young, he knows the place, he's up for anything, and he's *blood.*

So we go to dinner at the sushi place on Sunset, where he shows the Maine kid the glitz and the glamour. I'm having this great sushi and just drinking *everything,* building the world's greatest hangover.

And the more we drink, the further we go down memory lane remembering the good times with the family; how every Christmas we cousins would give the grandparents the same freaking gifts as the year before, and meanwhile there's my mom and his over in the corner sneaking more lobster with Chardonnay.

Sabe's grandfather John had just passed, so that was a big part of it. We talked openly, probably in a way we couldn't with anyone else, about the meaning of family, and how life is short, and how it's a big part of our job in life to look out for our elders.

And, yeah, also how insane it was that he and I have been out of touch for so long.

So all at once the idea was just out there: This is crazy, we should do something together!

I mean, that was the genesis—not *what* we'd do, but the wanting to do whatever it was together.

To be sure, part of the appeal was that both of us are entrepreneurial at heart, and while in our current jobs we both have a lot of autonomy, ultimately we're both working for other people.

Anyway, we now focus on the *what.*

Well, *duh.*

I mean, we're sitting there scarfing down sushi, but on this whole side of the country you can't find the other seafood delicacy we grew up with.

Because Sabin has looked. Sure, he tells me, if you walk into a steakhouse out here they might offer a surf-and-turf thing, a lobster tail and filet. But you won't find places, not even seafood restaurants, that do the lobster rolls we grew up with. And people out here don't know any better; they only know poor quality lobster, oftentimes mixed with sauces, chive, mayo, or other condiments to distract from the actual product quality.

In short, why not bring it out here and do it better? Drunk as we were, it didn't seem like rocket science. Because being from Maine, we *can* do it better than anyone else. We can tell the story—talk about the product and the lobstermen—and we have the contacts to get the highest quality lobster.

By way of full confession, I should add that as we're getting into this over our sushi on Sunset Boulevard, it is not lost on me that it's still snowing back in Boston, and I'll probably have to move to Cali.

Okay, we said, but maybe we should hit pause. I mean, it all sounds good, but we should at least consider other options. So we do for a little while. For instance, maybe we could do Amatos, the Italian sandwich that's a big thing in Maine—ham, cheese, lettuce, tomato, pickle, olive oil. Fabulous, both of us we grew up scarfing them down! Then, again, weren't they just a local variation of what you'd find in New York, and lots of other places? Wouldn't that by definition greatly limit its appeal?

That conclusion wasn't rocket science, either.

I mean, these days we have friends with burger trucks, and taco trucks, and pizza trucks, and while most do okay, some get pissed off that we always have long lines at our places and they don't, like we're practicing some kind of black magic. Well, they're good guys and they work hard, so I don't want to be harsh, but it's obvious you can get a burger or a pizza pretty much anywhere in LA. I mean, it's as if we decided to open up a lobster place in Maine, surrounded by competition.

Anyway, by the sixth or eighth drink we've decided it's definitely lobster, and we're both flying, batting notions back and forth about how it'll work.

"Okay, we'll have to get a shipment flown out every day . . ."

"Correct. Maximum freshness, that's probably the biggest selling point."

"How much you think we'll need—forty pounds a week? Fifty?"

"No idea. We'll figure it out."

The obvious first thought was a restaurant, probably a variation on the seafood shacks we have back home, only maybe a little classier. Then, again, wouldn't that involve a major financial commitment up front? And where would that come from?

"How about a food truck?" said Sabin.

"What's a food truck?" I'd literally never heard of them. We didn't have them yet in Boston.

"They're getting to be a big thing out here. Food on wheels."

"Oh, yeah?"

"Fuck it, we'll figure that part out."

I mean, literally from the very start, neither of us regarded our total ignorance of the food business, or business in general, as an impediment. It didn't even give us momentary hesitation.

In fact, in a curious way it was a great strength. Because little as we knew about business, the one thing we did know, beyond question, was one another's character. We knew that, tough and competitive as we both were, together we'd make it work, representing both our family and the state of Maine.

And that wasn't just because of the alcohol.

CHAPTER 4

Playing Chef

WE ARE CHEFS!!!

SABIN

The honest truth? After Jimmy left, I kind've forgot about the whole thing. I mean, I've got a really busy life, and I'm not drunk anymore.

So when he calls a few days later, with, "Hey, what do you think about that idea?" I was like, "Yeah, well, I don't know," because now it didn't sound nearly as good.

But he's not someone who gives up. He keeps calling, hammering away at it. *We gotta do it, we gotta do it!* And when I ignore this, he starts sending Excel docs laying out how if we sell just thirty lobster rolls a day, we'll break even, and all this other stuff.

And I keep on ignoring him; I won't even answer his calls. And when he texts, I won't answer those either. But the guy was relentless; you could drive a stake through his heart and he wouldn't stop.

He was so persistent that finally, *finally*, I agreed. Because by now I'd reached the same realization he had the first night. That my cousin may be the most incredibly annoying person in the world, but he has so much drive and crazy tenacity that he will *never* let this thing fail.

So fuck it, I tell him I'm in.

So now what? Because in the bright light of day, not only do neither of us know the first thing about running a business, but we're talking about a business where your only product is highly perishable and is on the other side of the country.

Obviously we're gonna have to do major research, and a whole lot more talking before plunging into this thing, which will also give us some time to see how well we actually click as partners. Because we know full well how fundamentally different we are in our thinking: Jimmy's far more analytical and by the book. He's an Excel sheet kind of guy, while I'm a more flamboyant, shoot-from-the-hip, let's-see-what-happens kind of guy. Moreover, presented with a problem,

Jimmy will keep smashing his head into the wall as many times as it takes to break through to the other side; while I'll smash my head a couple of times and then say, *fuck it*, this isn't worth it, and then find another route.

Over the years this will turn out to be a great combination, with my pushing him toward greater flexibility and risk-taking and him putting the brakes on my wilder flights of fancy. Eventually it would even lead to a natural division of responsibilities within the company.

But neither of us knew that yet.

Still, it didn't take long to begin discovering it—or actually *re*discovering it. For as we did our preliminary research on opposite sides of the country, comparing notes on everything, we remembered how well we got along even when we disagreed (which wasn't all that often, anyway); how straightforward we both are; how neither of us is a blamer or any kind of excuse maker; and in general just how much fucking fun we had being together.

Not that we were taking any chances. Just to be even surer, we actually took a personality assessment test. Why? Because bad as it would be for it to fail as a business venture, the one thing we absolutely couldn't risk was that it might screw up the family.

Of course, the test only further confirmed that we complemented each other perfectly.

The first major thing we had to decide was whether to go with a truck or brick and mortar. Food trucks were starting to get big in LA, but the concept was still alien to Jimmy, so for a little while we flirted with going the traditional route—which, frankly, also had the appeal of seeming more respectable and higher end. So I checked out some small restaurants in San Diego. But once we saw all the costs involved, and all the scary shit that comes with a lease, including personal guarantees, it was no contest. By then we'd learned we could get a used truck for fifty or sixty grand, meaning we'd each have to put in around $25,000, and that would be it. If it panned out, which we were sure it would, great; if not, we could recoup most of our investment by selling the truck.

At the same time, we saw the potential downsides for a truck, starting with the fact that restaurant interests in LA were fighting tooth and nail to get them banned. Then, too, there was the fact that, hot as they were at the moment, LA being LA, the food truck scene could fizzle out any time. Crazy as that sounds today, when even big brands like Chick-fil-A, In-N-Out Burger, and Wendy's have trucks on the road, in 2012 it was a real concern.

Anyway, we overcame those doubts. It ended up being a brilliant decision, because a food truck proved a perfect fit for our model. But we didn't do it because we were brilliant, we did it because it was cheaper and involved less exposure.

So now I began systematically checking out the food truck scene, keeping tabs on various trucks—steak trucks, cheese trucks, taco trucks, burger trucks—to see how many covers they did at different times and locations. I'd count their tickets and note how many people bought what, as well as seeing what percentage of potential customers ended up actually buying as opposed to just looking. Eventually we took all this data and calculated that all we needed to do to break even was sell only about thirty lobster rolls a day, just like Jimmy'd found in his Excel doc.

We already knew we weren't gonna cut any corners on quality. That was not so much a choice as a guiding philosophy. We'd source only the best, most expensive Maine lobster, and we'd treat customers with respect—in short, provide the full Maine experience.

That said, beyond lobster rolls, which would obviously be our centerpiece, we still had to figure out the menu. The fact is, at this point we're young guys who don't actually know our way around the kitchen. I cook for myself maybe one night a week, and the other six I eat out. On the plus side, this makes me an expert in what I want when I eat out, which is basically two things. One, the food has to be awesome, and two, the customer service has to be awesome. If either of those things is lacking, that's it, I'm never going back. So, again, that was going to be Cousins Maine Lobster's guarantee and our calling card.

As for the food . . . well, a few months in, Jimmy flies back to LA so we can nail down the menu. Of course, it's all out of pocket, and like me, he's also got a job, so this will be his only trip out prior to our actual launch. He's sleeping on an air mattress in my living room.

We know the lobster roll is going to be the basic element, but—this is how stupid we were—we haven't figured out if we want to start out just with lobster meat or have entire lobsters shipped out from Maine, like actual shells and bodies, because our thinking was we'd use the shells to create our own roux and make lobster bisque.

Like, what were we thinking? For one thing, there'd be no consistency, because you could never make sure it would be the same in every truck—not that at that point we were thinking of more than one truck—and for another, the very thought of flying lobster bodies three thousand miles to make a roux for a bisque was ridiculous. Speaking of which, we also figured we were going to make our own chowder from scratch, until we realized that we were gonna have to find a workaround for that, also.

Anyway, it was all trial and error in my one-bedroom place, with our main focus on figuring out *which* lobster meat works best for the rolls. A lot of people will say the tail is their favorite, but that's only because they're probably used to surf and turf. Actually the tail is a little tougher, and in our experiments we found there are other issues with using it in a roll. Tail meat is longer, for one thing, 2 to 3.5 inches, so to fit properly in the roll it has to be cut up, split in half, and diced; otherwise when you bite halfway into the roll, you'll probably pull the whole thing out and have an empty roll. Whereas if you use meat of the claw or knuckle, it's not only more tender and less stringy, you'll easily get just the size you need for a mouthful.

Very soon we also learn that meat from lobsters weighing between one and one and a half pounds is sweeter and more tender. People assume bigger is better, and obviously larger lobsters will have more meat in them. But the shell is harder, so the meat tends to be tougher and dryer.

Anyway, we're in my kitchen off and on for a couple of weeks, trying this meat and that, and working with different rolls. Because we're in California, we play around with lobster tacos and lobster ceviche—both will eventually be on the menu.

But what our experimenting mainly leads us to is an emphasis on simplicity. Once we have the lobster roll down, everything else is secondary. And even the lobster rolls are pretty basic. They have lobster, bread, and butter. That's it. One of them has a little mayonnaise, and another has warmed butter. There's no secret process. There's no chutney or paprika. It's literally lobster and bread. The fact is, it's not hard to copy our business. But the reason we've been so successful is that we've always sourced the best quality, and we don't deviate from that when prices get astronomical.

That, and the fact that we provide Downeast Maine hospitality. We're not gonna be stuffy but genuinely kind and thankful, where we'll tap people on the shoulder and thank them for coming in, and mean it.

Again, obvious, yet you'd be amazed how many places in Los Angeles don't do it.

JIM

Don't Overthink It

So, backtracking a bit, the morning after we come up with the idea, I wake up on an air mattress in Sabin's living room with the most extreme hangover ever, then fly back to Boston. For the next fourteen months it's like I have two jobs. I'm on my med device job from seven to seven, a twelve-hour day, then come home to the North End in Boston and head to Starbucks, pull up my computer and get out my notepads, and go to work on the lobster idea. I research sourcing of goods and shipping costs, potential menu items, all sorts of things until now I've known nothing about. I also take several trips to Maine to reestablish old contacts and create new ones.

I'm doing all this on my own time, making absolutely sure it's not interfering with Job One.

Which is to say, even as the lobster idea is getting more and more real, I'm not taking any chances. Exciting as it is, I'm still not completely, 100% committed.

It takes a few months before I go to my bosses—just in case they catch wind of anything—and let them know I'm looking into this thing with my cousin. And, in fact, having once been entrepreneurs themselves, they're cool with it. I also tell some of the doctors with whom I'm close.

Back in LA, Sabe has been hunting down food trucks, getting data on what's selling, and where, and for how much. The guy's a master BS-er, and I could just picture him jabbering away with the guy at the window (once he's made sure the guy's an employee, not the owner), and getting all kinds of possibly proprietary information. "Oh man, you guys are so busy today. Do you do any advertising? Social media? How many tickets you sold? Two hundred! Wow, and would this be an average day? So what's the breakdown between lunch and dinner?"

Once we've accumulated all this research, the next step—which is also a *psychological* leap—is for me to put together the menu. In a way it's a travesty—talk about a pair of babes in the woods—but in the end I think our inexperience also works to our advantage. Because after a week or ten days of playing chef in Sabe's six-hundred-square-foot apartment, messing around with live lobster, steaming them and picking out the meat, with the smell stinking up the place, the conclusion becomes obvious: What the hell are we thinking? What we're doing is hard enough, why layer on more complexity? And even if we wanted to do all the cooking and meat picking involved with having a broader range of products, the truck won't be large enough, anyway.

All we need is meat and rolls. That's it.

Because while we can show a twenty-two-year-old kid just hired off Craigslist how to put lobster in a bun, we don't even wanna try teaching him how to make a complex sauce.

Yes, we want great food, but we also want great speed and great efficiency, great ticket times and minimizing of cost, and as little waste as possible. We're not gonna be like other restaurants, where they make a whole bunch of shit and there's leftovers at the end of the day.

So by the end of my stay, we've thrown out the idea of making our own lobster roux or bisque (from the leftover bodies of the steamed whole lobsters we're not going to have!). We don't want to overcomplicate things. If we focus on the best lobster meat, we can apply it in many menu items, be it our traditional lobster rolls, or our lobster tacos, lobster tots, or lobster quesadillas.

I'll find other key vendors back in Maine. There's whoopie pies—classic Maine dessert. They already come in a plastic wrap, so all we'll need to do is hand them out the window. (There's another dessert item from a place in Maine—lobster ice cream, which actually tastes like poached lobster and butter—and we'll also try that for a while, if only because it's buzzworthy.) Our chowder and bisque will also come to us from the East Coast, ready made, packaged in a bag with our recipe; all we'll have to do is put them in a pot of boiling water, scoop, and fill. We'll also carry tots—our version of french fries—put the lobster meat and some pico de gallo on top of a pile of them, presto, you've got terrific pub food, shareable and filling.

Efficiency and speed, everything built around the roll. Once that's the focus, everything else falls into place.

At the end of my week in LA, we send out for a bunch more meat, and invite around twenty of Sabe's buddies, both guys and girls, over to his place—not all at once, but staggering them over a couple of hours. We toast up a bunch of buns, put the meat in there—no lettuce, no chive, nothing crazy to take away from the taste—and it's *Okay, what do you guys think?* And the overwhelming response was: *Holy shit, this is amazing!* We've got his Persian and Armenian buddies there, but also some New England transplants. This one girl from Scarborough, Maine, can hardly believe it, she's like *My God, this is SO good, EXACTLY like home!* So it was a great litmus test, and by the end we're pumped. We're definitely gonna do this, there's no way it won't work!

Back home, I now take on in earnest the task that will, or feels like it will, definitively lock us in: getting a truck. It turns out to be a lot harder than I expected. Finding one was problem enough, but the real issue was financing. It costs $65,000, and when I call lenders for loans I hear the same objections over and over: *Who are you? You've got no business history.* Or *You're not a chef or a restaurateur, you've got zero experience in food!* Or a few times it would be almost exactly my reaction to Sabin when the idea first arose: *What the hell IS a food truck?*

Finally, somewhere between my twenty-fifth and thirtieth call, I get a yes.

The truck is pretty basic, a used Freightliner. But it was formerly a Cape Cod Chips truck, which we take to be a great omen. In fact, Cape Cod Chips will end up being the chip we decide to sell.

We already know how we'll want it to look; this is one thing we've discussed in great detail. Because it's clear to us that the branding part is huge and that most food truck owners, either because they don't think about it or do and have lousy taste, screw it up. Even the ones that turn the sides of their trucks into artistic murals to make them look pretty. Because what's the message? *What the fuck are you selling?* You want people to buy your food? Tell them what it is.

And do it with attitude!

So when we ship our truck out to California for rewrapping, we make it jet black. Why? Because when we were kids playing sports, teams in black always seemed tough. I mean, as a hockey player, you'd see the other team skate onto the ice in black uniforms, and you were immediately intimidated.

Next, on both sides, against the black, we put a big red lobster and our name so big that even if we're at a big event—say, at Santa Anita racetrack, where there's fifty trucks in the infield—the eyes of every person in the grandstand will be drawn to that truck, and they'll have a very clear understanding of who we are and what we're selling.

When someone spots this thing coming down a regular city street, it'll be even better. It'll look like a rolling version of the old Oakland Raiders, and no one will miss what that means: We're Cousins from Maine. We're serving lobster, and we fucking mean business!

CHAPTER 5

Onto the Streets

OUR 1ST CUSTOMER

SABIN

Friday, April 27, 2012

The day we've been working and aiming at for fourteen months.

We'll be opening in the community of Artesia, in southeast LA—specifically, in the parking lot of a local community center with a listed starting time of 5 PM.

Why this particular spot in Artesia? No clue. Serving the area's large Portuguese American population, it's one of those places where people naturally congregate—a meeting hall, with lots of greenery outside. But, honestly, it could've been any of dozens of venues.

Basically, it's just another sign we're flying by the seat of our pants.

My advance PR has consisted of a single tweet saying *Hey, come out and join us Friday, get some fresh Maine lobster in Artesia.* I included a photo of me and Jim as kids with my grandfather on the rocks in Maine, holding up lobsters.

At the time I have a grand total of about sixty Twitter followers, all of them actual friends and acquaintances.

Jimmy's come back to LA for about four or five days, and now he'll only be here until tomorrow. Not yet ready to go all in, he's more or less playing hooky. When his boss calls, he tells him he's running a little late because he's stuck on the Tobin Bridge, back in Boston.

For all the time put into working on the project, not wanting any negativity, it's only in the past week that we've let our friends and family know about it. We hadn't wanted to risk any negative feedback. And, sure enough, what we mainly get is not so much enthusiasm as bewilderment. My friend Shaun, for instance, who's not a guy who shrinks from a challenge—he's a competitive soccer player—has a typical response. "Dude, a food truck? You're an actor, what the fuck do you know about the food business?"

It's not like we needed reminders that we're amateurs. In fact, we soon find that for all our planning, there are major things we haven't given nearly enough thought in advance of our debut. Starting with staffing the truck. We've squeezed ten people into our converted piece-of-shit truck, most recruited within the past few days from Craigslist. We figured that if those summer shacks back in Maine can run using high school kids as seasonal help, it should be a snap telling adults how to do it. (But we *have* made it a priority of dressing them in brand-new T-shirts and hats.)

What else? We've forgotten to bring the cash register.

Also, since the POS truck's generator is acting up, we're running late.

But we *do* have the lobster. Fifty pounds on ice. It arrived at LAX this morning and was delivered to our commissary right on time.

And, no question, the truck *looks* great! As it barrels down the 405 freeway, Jimmy and I, following behind it in my Audi A4, can see other drivers react. And why wouldn't they—because this big black truck with the red cutout design on the side just looks so fucking cool.

So by the time we reach the freeway exit for Artesia we're feeling it. All we have to do is sell thirty-five or forty rolls this evening at $12 each, and we'll be on our way! And if we continue at that pace over thirty days, we'll make enough to cover our expenses.

But then we pull into the parking lot and—holy shit!—there's got to be sixty or seventy people waiting in line!

Immediately, I mean in that first second, I turn to Jim and go, "Oh man, this is gonna be really, *really* big!"

It takes another half hour before we can open, because we've got to get the griddle going, and, yeah, because not one member of our crew is trained to flip over and toast and butter our little buns; and of course we don't have a butter wheel like we do now, so it all has to be done by hand. I mean, we had people that probably hadn't even held a knife before. So it's chaos in there, basically we're doing our training on the fly, and it's not like at that point we know what the hell we're doing ourselves.

Yet none of it matters. The people outside the truck are unbelievably patient, and there are more and more of them. Jim and I leave the truck to go outside, and we start handing out free samples because the food's taking too long, shaking people's hands to thank them for coming. Several tell us they've been to a lot of food trucks, but this is the first time they've met the owners. Which to Jim and me seems incredible, because where we're from, you always say thank you, and always shake someone's hand.

And then the window opens, the food comes out, and now they want to shake *our* hand. This is incredible, they tell us, it's way better than any lobster they've ever had before. Or they say that it brings back memories of growing up back east. Or they want to know when we're coming back, 'cause they have to tell their friends. And they're getting on line for a second roll, or a third.

Meanwhile more and more people keep showing up.

Only now do we learn there's a website called UrbanDaddy that tells people what's hot in LA that week, and somehow they'd seen my tweet and blasted it out as something that's hot that Friday.

At some point, I turn to Jimmy and say, "You cannot leave tomorrow! This is too huge, you cannot leave me!"

I mean, yeah, I know he's got his job, and the plan was we'd set up the shipments, break in the staff, and then he'd go back to Boston. But at that moment, astonished as I am at what's going on around us, I'm also terrified that I'm gonna be left on my own. I mean, the next two weeks are fully scheduled, and I've got to make sure we'll have enough lobster, and enough manpower, and all the rest of it. And I guess I'm even more terrified that he's not gonna stick with all this over the long term.

But I don't want to overstate my anxiety, because mainly the whole night's unbelievably positive. By the time we head home to my one-bedroom, it's close to midnight and both of us are completely fucking exhausted, but punched in the face with happiness.

Then we dump out all the cash on my coffee table and start counting. I swear to God, it looks like a drug deal.

And then we count again, to make sure.

We'd have been happy to bring in $300. There's more than seven thousand.

Thirty seconds later I wake up my buddy Shaun, back in New York.

"What the . . ."

"Listen, this is gonna be really, really, *really* big. You gotta come out here and do it with us!"

Meanwhile, Jim's popped open his computer. "Hey, we got an email from *Shark Tank*."

I don't even know what that is.

JIM

Flying by the Seat of Our Pants

In the run-up to the opening, the question—at least for me—was if we were ready to fully and wholeheartedly commit to Cousins Maine Lobster as our future or to regard this as an experiment that *might* turn into more.

I mean, absolutely, all the work I'd done helping us get this far had only confirmed my belief in the idea we'd hatched that drunken night, and I couldn't wait to see it go from the drawing board onto the streets.

But Sabin is already all in, amped up and gung ho, an engine in overdrive, utterly certain this thing will succeed. He can already see it, and if any problems arise they can go fuck themselves. I'm innately more conservative, my impulse is to feather the brakes and think through, or maybe overthink, the implications. Am I really ready to quit a job that I love, one that will provide a fully secure future, for a leap into the unknown? Am I really ready to leave behind my family and my life back east?

Speaking of which, I have one buddy whose dad, a higher-up at Staples, recently shared the fact that only one in thirty-seven new business startups will be a success.

I return to LA a week or so before the big day, and Sabe and I spend much of that time driving around town. Our purpose is to check out potential sales venues for the truck, places with good street traffic and property owners likely, for their own purposes, to have us in their parking lots. With the help of local contacts, Sabin has already set up sites for the first couple of weeks, but we will need many, many, many more.

So the exercise is at once exhilarating and more than a little daunting. All I'm seeing is the enormity of the task we've set for ourselves. Obviously, it's a given that Los Angeles is immense. But seeing the number of distinct communities, each with its own tastes and peculiarities, is nothing short of overwhelming.

We start in South Central, where we're housing our truck, and where it'll get restocked—Slauson Avenue, South LA—and Sabin's like, "Dude, keep your windows up and keep your eyes open." The place is just a gated, fenced lot with barbed wire on top, with a hundred food trucks parked inside. The whole place reeks, and there's a million seagulls flying around.

For this kid from Cape Elizabeth, Maine, it's quite a shock.

But then we drive ten minutes and we're looking at palm trees and beautiful plush grass, and we go twelve miles in another direction and we're watching celebrities ripping through Venice Beach, and the sun setting over the ocean.

Is this intelligence even valuable? I mean, it's not like there's much question that we're probably gonna do okay in Venice or Santa Monica or Beverly Hills. Presumably every other food truck in town knows the same thing.

But, again, at this point we don't yet know any of this, we're just getting the general lay of the land. And I'm still thinking about how much we don't know—from the cost of certain goods and what the payroll's gonna be, even the price of gas at the different venues, not to mention all the stuff we haven't even thought of yet.

Even the choice of Artesia for the opening was far from a sure thing; we were going there on the recommendation of a gal Sabin knows from Orange County who's been helping us out a few hours a week. A community center in a middle-class, ethnically diverse area does sound like a decent bet. Plus, it has the advantage of being far enough out of the way that if it's a quasi bust, the fallout will probably be limited.

So as Sabin and I follow the truck to the grand opening in his Audi, all this is in the back of my mind. Excited as I am, I'm also prepared for (and already rationalizing) the possibility of disappointment.

As in: What if no one shows up? What if they do but they don't like our lobster? Or like it okay, but not as much as what they're used to? Or what if they like the lobster but don't like it on the roll?

All of which of course leads to the most insistent one of all: Who are we to be starting a lobster business in the first place? I'm in medical device sales, Sabin's in real estate and acting, I was a political science major at Holy Cross, and, though he'll tell you he did, Sabin probably didn't even graduate Hofstra (I kid). Neither of us has even the slightest experience in food or hospitality.

But the answers start to come the moment we pull up at the location—and, incredibly, they're all the right ones.

Already there are fifty or sixty people waiting. It turns out the church has sent out an email alerting the parishioners that something called Cousins Maine Lobster will be there on Friday night, and we now also find out about the UrbanDaddy announcement.

It's immediately clear that fresh Maine lobster is as big a draw as we hoped.

As they wait, people are clearly *excited.* They gather at the menu displayed inside the truck, avidly studying the items: Maine lobster rolls (chilled, with a touch of mayo) or Connecticut rolls (warm, with butter and lemon) at $13; lobster tacos ($13); New England clam chowder and lobster bisque (each at $6 per cup, $8 per bowl); and for dessert, whoopie pie or—what's this?—*lobster ice cream*?

There are couples and families and bunches of friends, talking and laughing, and they couldn't be happier to wait a little longer.

And then the window finally opens and the money starts *flying* in. It's unbelievable, better than we ever could have imagined. Even more unbelievable, more people keep coming.

After a few minutes, Sabin comes up behind me, whispering in my ear, "When are you moving here? I can't do this alone! WHEN are you moving?"

I hesitate, but of course, if anything was ever gonna make me a believer, this is it. *Holy shit*, I'm thinking, *am I gonna do this?* I mean, this is literally AS I'm raking in cash and watching the food go out the window, exactly like we envisioned.

Still, even then there's that little voice going: *Yeah, but how much of it is profit? Who knows what we'll walk away with when we're done tonight?*

Well, the end comes—I mean, by now it's ten thirty or eleven—and we've not just exceeded expectations but left them in the dust. Sitting beside me on a bench, Sabe is hyperenergized, and he's got the actor thing in him going, so again he's like: "You gonna move, you've *got* to!"

So after a little while, late as it is, I call my parents back in Maine. I tell them about this incredible day, and that I'm seriously considering relocating here.

"Jim," says my dad, in that way of his, "don't get ahead of yourself. It's just day one. You have a full-time job in Boston that's secure and that you need to go back to. It pays your bills and with a food truck there's no guarantee."

Which of course makes all kinds of sense. At this juncture, we've barely even considered what it will take to sustain the operation over the long haul, let alone to grow it. We'd succeeded that day only by flying by the seat of our pants. We'd ordered one hundred pounds of lobster, but that was sheer guesswork, we hadn't run projections; we'd only hoped it would be enough. And of course while we knew we could order more for the next day, the day after that would be Sunday, so if we ran out of meat then, we just wouldn't be able to go out.

Which obviously is no way to run a business. But we didn't know enough then to realize even *that*. In fact, we *liked* selling out; we were *proud* of it. Insane, I know now—'cause if lobster's your whole business, why would you *ever* sell out? It's like a brewery being happy to run out of beer. Yes, it's perishable, but we should at least be keeping enough on hand to cover Sundays.

Anyway, then Sabin and I go back to his place, where, to save money, I've been sleeping on his air mattress. And now the big moment. We throw all the money on this square, half-wood, half-glass table in his living room, and it's like we're swimming in cash. We're both ecstatic.

I mean, it's beyond fantastic. And this in spite of our inexperience. We don't even have a business bank account, we don't know what a P&L looks like, but we're still sitting there counting and recounting a ton of cash.

Finally, exhausted, I'm trying to go to sleep, but Sabin's still on a high. He's on the phone with his buddy Shaun, telling him about it, and that *he* has to join us out here.

So sitting on my air mattress, I pop open my laptop.

"Hey, Sabe, look at this!"

"What?" He's off the phone now.

"We got an email from *Shark Tank*!"

"Oh, yeah?" A beat. "What the hell is *Shark Tank*?"

"You kidding me?"

But no, he's not. So I give him a quick rundown on the show—how guys like us pitch their startups to a bunch of successful entrepreneurs, and hopefully one of the entrepreneurs backs them in exchange for a piece of the company.

The email, from one of the show's producers, is not exactly an offer to put us on the air, more like wanting to know if we're interested in auditioning. But it also makes clear that if we are, we'll get to circumvent the usual process and jump to the head of the line. It seems she was at the event, and never said a word to us, but she loved the food, loved the concept, and thinks we'll be a great fit.

Talk about the cherry on top of an unbelievable day! Here's this kid from Maine in Los Angeles, where all the glamour supposedly happens, and it's actually happening to *us*!

Of course, it helps that I know of the show—to this day I still watch it with my wife—whereas Sabin has no clue. So for him it's not nearly as big a deal.

Having finished day one, he's already on to thinking about day two, tomorrow, and the next two weeks, which are already booked and scheduled. And after that there will hopefully be months and years and, who knows, even decades of days to come.

"So we should do this, right?" I say.

He shrugs. "Probably. Why not?"

And that's how we reply to them, just not in those words.

CHAPTER 6

Saying No (and Yes) to *Shark Tank*

JIMMY + STEVE, 1990

SABIN

I wasn't just being my smart-ass self, I really hadn't heard of *Shark Tank*. I don't watch much TV to start with, and when I do it's mainly sports.

But, anyway, we get in touch with them the next day, and they set up a full conversation for a few days after that.

When the call happens, Jim and I are both in South Central, overseeing the truck getting restocked, but we've decided it's best to take the call in different places. So while we're talking to the *Shark Tank* people, he's in his car parked outside the commissary, with the doors locked and the seagulls making their racket, and I'm sitting in mine on the next block.

And by now we've already had second thoughts.

Because, just starting out as we are, beyond the thrill of being on TV, we can't see what's in it for us or the company.

The conversation is pleasant enough, but it doesn't do much to change our minds. Yes, it's nice to know they've never before done a food truck, and that startups involving food usually do well on the show. We take it all in with interest. But if we go on the air and tell millions of people our genius idea, what's to keep someone from copying us? And what's our pitch to the sharks, *Hey, we've done four days of sales, and it's going great!*? What value can we ask? What equity can we give?

Bottom line: We'll look like the idiots we are, and then they'll go to a commercial.

Besides which, we actually don't even need their money. The business seems like it's going to explode, and we have savings, so, why do this?

The next day we give them the verdict: Thanks but no thanks.

They're surprised—I mean, there are thousands of people dying to do the show—but they're gracious about it. They only ask that we keep an open mind to the idea, which is easy enough to agree to.

Anyway, it's already looking like our big concern will not be drumming up more business but making sure we have enough lobster, and enough manpower, for the business that's coming.

And it turns out we're not wrong about that.

The following days are a blur, but in terms of sales they're pretty much like the first day. And it's really never stopped—we've been running uphill for the past fourteen years.

No exaggeration, we go overnight from nonexistent to being the biggest thing in Los Angeles. Anywhere our truck is due to appear, there's three hundred people waiting. I mean, *every* time, *every* place. We go to Venice; we go to Burbank; we're in Santa Monica; we're in Beverly Hills. We can literally go anywhere and be successful.

The first month, we do roughly $85,000 in sales. The second month $150,000. We never for a moment have to be concerned with breaking even. We were always making serious money.

I'm not saying it's easy. It's nonstop; we're working our asses off. Especially since, yes, we both still have our other jobs. I'm in LA, juggling a million things, and Jimmy's constantly flying back and forth between the coasts. It's insanity.

It's not like I'm keeping anything from my bosses—as if I could!—and, anyway, they're incredibly supportive. Just very, very happy for me. In fact, when they see the truck in person, and the lines, one of them, Lio, tells me: "You need a second truck, and you need it immediately!" And I'm like, No way! He may as well be telling me I need to open a restaurant on the moon. Because I don't have the time for that. As it is, I can't even fucking sleep.

Meanwhile, Jimmy has his own situation. He not only has a really good job, with benefits—which mine doesn't—but he'll have to move out here. And his whole life, his family, and all his friends are on the East Coast.

I mean, he at least has to consider the possibility that it could turn out to be just a flash in the pan. It's not exactly news that LA loves the hot new thing, But after a while, that hot club isn't packed anymore, and that hot restaurant isn't so busy. Are we going to be able to sustain this thing and continue to grow it, especially with the brick-and-mortar restaurants fighting to get rid of food trucks altogether? Who knows, it's possible the whole scene could fizzle out in a year or two.

A few weeks in, I happen to have a talk with Jim's dad, Steve. He's an accountant, and he asks how we're doing financially.

Me: "Oh, we're doing great."

Steve: "Well, how's your P&L look?"

Me: "What's a P&L?"

Steve: "Your profit and loss statement. How are you determining how much money you're making?"

Me: "I don't need that. I got a bank account, I just look at that."

Because it's a cash business, with all these tens and twenties and fifties flooding in every day, up 'til now I've just been going to our local bank and sticking them in a checking account. And that's working fine. If Jim or I need to pay for something, we just take fifty bucks from the till, and never give it a second thought.

Steve, to his credit, does not go haywire when he hears this. That's not his personality—he's the most straightforward, rational person you'll ever meet. He just calmly explains that if we want to start doing it right, we can't run it like cowboys. We're going to get financially disciplined and start thinking about payroll taxes and income taxes and all this other shit.

"Listen," he says, "it's pretty simple, you're going to need to decide now if you want to run a mom-and-pop shop—where you don't pay sales tax, you hide your money, you pay your employees in cash—or do you want to run a real business. And if you want to run a business—and if one day you might want to sell the business—you have to do it the right way now. Not to mention, if you go on *Shark Tank*, which I understand you've been considering, and you get a deal, you're going to have to show you run it like a business, because you'll have a partner."

Well, I don't tell him this, but to me, at least, it sounds a lot more intriguing to run the business dirty—to hide money and not pay sales tax and all that cowboy shit.

And Jim and I actually discuss doing that.

But Jim is more like his dad, and although we really don't want to—at least I don't—we end up listening to Steve.

Obviously it's the smartest thing we ever did—and, right there, shows the difference between having a dad in your background and not.

So we end up doing it the right way, and lo and behold, today we're running a $100 million-a-year business, with over a billion dollars in sales, and a $15 million line of credit.

When we do finally decide to go on *Shark Tank*, we're able to answer their questions with at least some semblance of not being total jackasses, and leaving at least some impression, however mistaken, that we know what the fuck we're doing.

STEVE TSELIKIS

I don't specifically recall that conversation, but it sounds about right. I'd certainly recognize the appeal to someone like Sabin of doing it on his own terms, and maybe bending the rules a little. When I was a kid, in my neighborhood the guys at the corner stores selling sandwiches and pizzas always had their cash registers open—they never wanted to ring anything up and leave a record of a transaction. All they wanted to know was how much money do I have.

So I'm actually sympathetic to that way of operating. And I know it goes hand in hand with the kind of chaotic, undisciplined childhood Sabin had. It's just not the way to build a serious business—which I think both the guys understood.

It's funny, I actually don't recall the two of them being particularly close growing up. We'd only really get together as a family on special occasions, like holidays, and that three-year age gap made a huge difference when they were young. It wasn't anything malicious, but Jim tended to get excluded. I get that. My brother's five years older, and in some ways I went through that too.

They're also strikingly different people. I realize that from seeing them on TV and the company name, a lot of people lump them together as a couple of guys from Maine, but in their personalities and approaches to life, they could hardly be more dissimilar. Sabin is an extrovert; he's naturally flamboyant. It makes perfect sense that he was going to have an acting career, and it's something his mother fostered—I think she was gonna be his agent. And while Jim has now become much more amenable to meeting new people and opening up in conversation, because he's had to, it's not his basic nature. He's more introspective, and nowhere near the ham Sabin is.

So I guess when Jim first told his mother and me about this idea the two of them had worked up of selling lobster from a truck in

LA, it was a bit of a surprise. Still, it was presented as no big thing, sort of a whim—just a way to maybe make a few extra bucks. They weren't going to work it themselves, they'd hire other people to do that. I mean, they both had decent jobs and were making reasonably good money, Sabin doing real estate stuff out there, and Jim selling medical supplies in the Boston area. Besides, neither of them had studied business in school or had any hands-on experience in the business world.

Basically, at that point it was more like they were just continuing that conversation that started over drinks.

But I had to give them credit that they went ahead and actually launched the business. And once they put the thing on the road, everything changed.

I think they were as stunned as anyone by the response to the opening day. And it was just like Sabin to react with: Let's go open up five hundred more!

And like Jim to be more hesitant and want to take more time before going all in.

As for his mother and me, we had completely different thoughts about him quitting his job and giving this a try. She was really fearful about the whole venture and skeptical about the idea of selling lobster from a truck. But I thought about my own work history, where the longest-term job before I finally settled in at Goodwill Industries was maybe three or four years.

After graduating with a psych degree from a local Maine college, I went to work for the state in that field. But I tired of that pretty quickly and decided I wanted to go into business, so I went back to college for business and accounting and became a CPA. I worked in public accounting for three years, got tired of that, and then worked for a consortium of Maine banks; and then I left that to go to work for a real estate developer. Goodwill only came at the end of all that.

So my attitude now was to give it a shot. They were both young, not married, no family, no ties—if they're ever going to do it, this is the time. They could take the risk because they could afford to fail. And in Jim's case, if it was a disaster, I was confident he could have gone back to selling medical supplies.

The main thing was not ever to have to look back and wish they had.

And right from the beginning, I was impressed by how well they meshed as partners. I don't know how, because it's not formalized—there's no organizational structure that says here's what you do, here's what I do—but somehow they have a division of responsibilities that avoids disagreements and tripping over each other. They can both be strong willed, but they just work that stuff out. And part of it is their shared history lets them to talk to each other with an ease and humor that business partners usually never would.

They'll banter, and get on each other's case, and *no subject* is ever off-limits. They'll say things to each other that no one else would; it's part of how they relate. For instance, it's a running joke between them how Sabin's always looking to latch on to a father figure, so every so often they'll be at some random gathering, and Jim will nudge him and whisper, "Hey, is that your father over there?" And Sabin gives plenty as good as he gets. They can do it because that's how close they are.

From the company's inception, when they had only the one truck in LA, I assumed the accounting and bookkeeping responsibilities. And I stayed in that position for four or five years, until we farmed it out to an outside accounting firm that Sabin knew from his earlier work with the real estate guys. So we don't have in-house accounting services. There's only me more or less overseeing the consulting firm and the overall financial end.

And of course, standing ready to offer advice if asked. I don't know how useful it is—probably a lot less now, since they've learned so much since the beginning. But I'm available.

That's one thing you never retire from: being a parent.

JIM

Be Different

At this point, when I'm in LA, which is more and more often, I'm spending just about every waking hour setting up bookings. Without them, there's no business. The only time you *don't* have to book a location is if you're in an isolated dirt parking lot somewhere, in which case that day you're acting as a pop-up storefront and trying to figure out ways to drive people to you.

So I'm picking up every bit of information I possibly can, then going and following up. Finding out, say, what kind of business does that liquor store with the big adjacent parking lot do between 5 PM and 8 PM on an average Friday; and whether it's that busy because most of the people stopping off to get their booze there are en route to their weekend houses?

And, then, if everything checks out, how amenable is the owner to having us in the lot, part of the negotiation having to do with the likelihood we'll be bringing a fair number people to him? And if that works, maybe we'll arrange to come back every second or third week.

Multiply that by fifty or so places a month, including churches, farmers' markets, gas stations, and hardware stores. Then, too, there are festivals and music and art events, though we're learning they will often try and charge 20% of our proceeds, meaning we have to increase the price on our lobster rolls to offset it. But the bonus is you get a lot of people in an isolated area.

Anyway, in the midst of all this frenetic activity, Sabe and I decide we might as well at least do an audition tape for *Shark Tank*—what they call a "pitch video." The idea is to display our personalities and give some sense of how we'll play on TV. So we do one that runs a couple of minutes, totally unscripted, basically we just toss it off.

Later we hear that's exactly what they like about it, especially one particular moment. We're at a food truck event, and the guy with the camera's like "Do something stupid," so I lift up my T-shirt and start doing tricep kickbacks with a Maine Root soda bottle, while apologizing to *Shark Tank* for doing it. It's so different from the tapes most people send in, where they're trying to come off as serious businesspeople, all buttoned up and formal as they describe their products or companies, that it immediately stands out. I looked like an idiot, but it did the trick.

So of course now they want us to do the show more than ever.

We hesitate, then kind of agree, then we pull back again, always for the same basic reason: *Why* Shark Tank*?*

All right, in hindsight we're complete idiots. Still, we're selling lots of lobster rolls and have as much work as we can handle—in fact, *more*, since we also still have our other jobs.

Then a week or so later, we get *another* call, this one from Yun Lingner, the show's executive producer. Sabin's in LA and I'm now back in Boston. It's later on the East Coast, and it's raining, and I've just gone into a bar near Beacon Hill with my buddies when the call comes. Which is cool, 'cause I get to say, "Hey, guys, like I gotta dip out of this bar to talk to the executive producer of *Shark Tank*."

I'm under an awning while it's pissing rain out, and she makes her strongest pitch to Sabe and me. Which was similar to the others, until the end of the conversation, when she tells us straight out that if we don't do this we'll be making "the biggest mistake of your lives."

So she gets off and Sabe and I talk, trying to be levelheaded, talking over the pros and cons. We're like, okay, it could be for the sake of the spectacle, she could just be trying to get us on for their own selfish interests. Like look at these two young kids, with their fucking food truck, what a joke! Or it could really be they've never had a food truck, and they truly believe it's an up-and-coming thing. Or that they like the idea of lobsters. And, hey, maybe *because* we have no idea what we're doing, we'd actually be good on TV. You know, blah, blah, blah, because we had no idea.

The upshot is, we decide we'll take a roll of the dice. Finally, we say yes.

But, still, it's not like our concerns have disappeared. In fact, now we have a new one. After all, up to now we've called all the shots. But this thing's a total crap shoot, there are all kinds of elements we can't control. What if we're on the show and we give the sharks lobster samples, and for some reason the lobster doesn't taste right? Or what if it hasn't been heated properly? Or, hell, what if Mark Cuban is just in a bad mood that day? Now we'll have ten million people hearing our food is crap!

What if not a single one of them makes us an offer???

So we almost pull out again. In fact, we'll keep going back and forth almost 'til the last minute.

CHAPTER 7

On Camera

HOLY SHIT, WE DID IT!

YUN LINGNER

(Executive Producer, *Shark Tank*)

The beauty of *Shark Tank* is that it's a really simple format; in the end, it all hinges on the quality of the entrepreneurs. At this point, we get literally thousands of submissions a year, some from online submissions and open calls. But we also do what we call cherry-picking, going out to businesses that have caught our eye and asking them if they're interested in applying. That's because we want the show to reflect the times, with every season a reflection of what's going on in the culture generally, in terms of interests and trends.

For instance, AI is of interest now, so we'll see if there are any cool, interesting AI businesses out there. Though how they come to us has no bearing on whether they'll ultimately get on the show; in those cases we'll reach out and ask if they want to apply.

Cousins Maine Lobster was one of those.

As executive producer, I've pretty much done the same thing for the entire existence of *Shark Tank*, starting with the pilot episode. Since 2012 was Season Four, fairly early on in its history, I was doing a little bit more cherry-picking than I might today.

In that regard, the first season had been the hardest, since nobody knew what the show was. Was it about actual sharks? That was one of the reasons that first season didn't get much notice, and as a result, we got only a small order for the second season, only eight episodes. At that point, most networks probably would have canceled us, but ABC believed in the vision and took a chance on the show.

And then, in the third season, we really hit. People became aware of what the show was, so casting became much easier; people started to get what a tremendous opportunity it was to win mentorship and investment from business heavy hitters they would otherwise not have access to—and for exposure to millions of people.

For the Cousins Maine Lobster guys, the timing—Season Four—was really fortuitous, because while it was still early days for the show, it was over the hump and starting to be the cultural phenomenon it would become.

And it was great timing in another way, for though food trucks are ubiquitous now, ten or twelve years ago they weren't commonplace. In fact, they were just starting to be a thing. I remember going to lunch near our office in Santa Monica, and coming across a little area with a bunch of food trucks. So I went over to investigate, and one of them was a lobster truck. In cherry-picking mode, I went over and got a lobster roll. And it was great!

The irony: It was NOT Cousins Maine Lobster.

I won't give the guy's name, but it was a different operation, different everything. So I reached out to the founder about trying out for the show and he was interested, and I passed the information along to our casting department.

What happened? I don't remember the details, but the upshot is that he ended up changing his mind.

But that experience had made me curious about the whole food truck concept, and I went online and googled "Lobster roll truck Los Angeles." An LA truck was preferable for logistic reasons, because we shoot in LA. Anyway, Cousins Maine Lobster's website came up; a nice-looking site, including a picture of the two handsome guys. But you could tell it was super early for the business; in fact, I'm pretty sure they hadn't even gone out for their first service yet.

I spoke to them on the phone, and we had a great conversation. They seemed charismatic and interesting and very interested in being on the show, so I passed them along to our casting department, and our casting director, Mindy Zemrak, who coincidentally is from Maine. She went to their opening and they were well on their way to being on the show.*

But then—somewhere in the process—they got cold feet and pulled out.

So it's basically the same story as the first guy. Except in that case the guy pulled out much earlier in the process, and I just let it go. But with these guys, I'd talked to them more and knew their story, and knew they'd be great on the air. I also knew what their hesitation was—and that it wasn't so much that they didn't want to do the show, as that it was super early for their company.

They were afraid if they came on the show, they wouldn't come off as super business savvy or have had enough sales; and that having just the one truck to talk about, their pitch to the sharks would be too thin. And the truth is, they had a point. If somebody came in today under those same circumstances, with the same resume, they probably wouldn't get on the show.

Anyway, the bottom line was that they were afraid if they did the show they would make fools of themselves and probably get ripped apart by the sharks along the way. Plus, they were thinking someone else could steal their idea, which was an altogether valid concern.

Well, normally I would totally just let it go, right? Because I totally understand their hesitation. I'm also sure they had a mistrust of reality TV in general, which is something else I completely understand.

So why didn't I let it go? Logically, I should have, because as a rule, entrepreneurs who are hesitant to do the show rarely work out

* NOTE: The discerning reader will note that Yun's recollection of events is somewhat at odds with our own. But since we love her, and are very much indebted to her and the show, we refuse to get into a pissing match. (But it *is* two against one.)

in the end anyway; there are just too many hoops to jump through to get from the audition to get on air—a ton of working on the pitch and everything else that goes into the presentation—and if you're not fully on board, it's going to show eventually.

It's not like we didn't have plenty of other people eager to be on the show.

So normally I never try to convince people. But in this case, there was just something that made me not want to let it go, just a feeling. For the first time, I called the prospective entrepreneurs, and basically told them *You know what, you NEED to do this. You're not gonna make fools of yourselves, and you're not gonna get shredded by the sharks.* Because I just didn't think that was going to happen.

I didn't know if they'd get an offer—it *was* super early, and the sharks might not be interested. But I knew they were charismatic, they were super likable, that they had a great story, and they'd be good for TV.

So I kind of talked them into it and they did it.

And, you know what, it was perfect timing. They were the right people to do it, they made a deal with the perfect shark, and it all just flowed from there. It ended up being an amazing thing that no one could have foreseen. I certainly had no idea myself this little food truck could turn into all that it has.

The way I look at it, *Shark Tank* was the spark, the opportunity; but a lot of people over the years have had the opportunity and didn't have the drive to take full advantage. So it's 100% all on them and Barbara. I'm just happy to have been that little bit of kismet that happened to get the ball rolling.

By the way, that other lobster truck? Honestly, I don't even remember the guy's name, but I know they're still in business, because I've seen them around. But I've never spoken to him, and I certainly would never want to seem to be rubbing it in.

SABIN

Now that we're committed, we go into intensive prep mode. We have to decide not just what we want to say to the sharks (and their millions of fans), but just as important, how we need to come off saying it. We know, or at least hope, that on the plus side we have youthful energy and charm going for us. The problem is, how to keep these business tycoons from nailing us on our other defining quality: our woeful inexperience.

Since Jim is still in Boston, we do it mainly on the phone, with long calls almost every night.

Meanwhile, we're both closely watching the show and taking lots of notes. One thing that's quickly apparent is that the sharks, at this time, consistently ask the same questions. "How did you come up with this valuation?"—that's one of the five that Mark Cuban is almost sure to ask. Barbara Corcoran asks her five, and Daymond John his five. So what we do is make flash cards with the questions on one side and our answers on the other—like we're in fucking middle school—and we then learn the answers word for word.

"Why lobster? What's so special about it?"

"What's the upkeep on the trucks?"

"What are your shipping costs?"

Literally anything any of them might ask.

All in all, we feel we're on pretty solid ground about the financials, since the results to date have been spectacular. On the other hand, we're only talking two months, and they'll definitely ask about the long term: The food scene is changeable; will this last? What if food trucks are just a passing fad? What if the cost of lobster goes through the roof? And since we basically agree with them about all that—and "We don't know" doesn't sound like a great answer—we know we have to hone our bullshitting skills in anticipation of those moments, which involves subtly shifting the focus to more manageable subjects like the endless booking opportunities and the quality of the lobster.

We also scour the internet for any little nuggets about the sharks themselves that may prove useful. For instance, we discover that Daymond once worked at Red Lobster—and, hey, that will actually come up in the episode.

Our biggest concern, the thing we figure might well screw us with the sharks before word one, is that we've only got one truck in one city. So, okay, it's nice the money's rolling in, but what kind of business model is that?

Even thinking about that conversation freaks us out, raising a familiar fear—that others elsewhere will copy us—and making us wonder all over again why we're doing the show.

In response, or desperation, we start tossing around the idea of adding another dimension to the business, something else to dangle in front of the sharks—an e-commerce component, where we'll ship items overnight from Maine to the customer's door. On investigation, it turns out there are three or four other operations back in Maine doing that already. But whatever, we'll do it anyway. Because how the hell are we gonna stand there for half an hour just talking about our one truck in Los Angeles?

A week before the taping Jimmy comes out to LA for the final phase of rehearsing, and this is where things get really intense. I devise this exercise where we sit face-to-face and quiz each other rapid fire, question-answer, question-answer. Immediately after that we turn and run out the door for a run through West Hollywood—fast enough so our heart rates rise to anxiety level—continuing to fire questions and answers as we go. Then, still running, we go into our opening pitch:

Sabin: My name is Sabin Lomac . . .

Jim: . . . and I am his younger cousin Jim Tselikis . . .

Together: . . . and together we are Cousins Maine Lobster!

Sabin: Sharks, we're here seeking $55,000 in exchange for 5% of our company.

Jim: Sharks, at Cousins Maine Lobster, we bring the Maine lobster experience to Southern California, and we do it via our amazing gourmet lobster shack on wheels.

People we pass think we're out of our minds, but that's also part of the point, to ignore them, like we do all the other distractions, from police sirens, to good-looking women, to the jerks bearing down on us on racing bikes. Focus is everything, and this is as close as we can create to the all-or-nothing atmosphere we'll face as we stand under bright lights, facing a bunch of ruthless billionaires.

Being an actor, I, at least, have faced a version of this before. But it's all new to Jim, and I can't let his nerves get the best of him. I tell him not to overthink it, just be himself, all the obvious stuff. But of course it's not as easy as it sounds, which is clear when you see how many people on that show screw it up. But Jimmy's not them; he's a hockey player, has always been a fast learner, and he takes on the challenge of being himself before millions of viewers with the same zeal he used to bring to the ice.

So finally we get to the point where the pitch is becoming almost second nature for both of us, and we're feeling ready for whatever the sharks throw at us.

And, in fact, when we tape the episode, there's a moment when that's tested. Mark Cuban is dismissing our valuation, basically saying we're greedy, and I realize he's about to use one of his pet expressions—that "80% of a watermelon is better than 100% of a grape." So even as he starts to say it, I beat him to it. "Mark, you said 5% of something is better than 0% of nothing in the past."

The viewer sees his surprise: having his own cliché thrown back at him. But it wasn't because I'm that smart, it's because I was really well prepared. Of course, going in we already have a good sense of the personalities of each of the sharks, and how they interact with one another.

On the other end of the spectrum, there's Barbara Corcoran, who's a straight shooter and seems very different than some of the others. She's kind of maternal, which is appealing, since we're both mama's boys; plus, unlike Cuban and some of the others who are in the prime of their careers, she's at the latter part of hers, so she'll probably be more hands-on.

So we decide to focus on Barbara.

Call it "research," but we find ways to speak with some of the other companies she's done deals with, like Kim Nelson over at Daisy Cakes. It confirms our impression of her that she's totally for real and extremely genuine.

The final element in our prep is the costuming. We decide to go native—*Maine* native, that is, the way we'd dress at one of the lobster shacks we used to go to as kids: shorts, flip-flops, and T-shirt. It fits the impression we want to convey both as people and food truck entrepreneurs, fun, relaxed, maybe a little . . . well, if not cocky, confident.

And now there's nothing left to do but do it.

JIM

Into the Tank

We're scheduled to shoot our episode in July 2012. The way it works is that the night before, they put you up in a hotel in Culver City, close to the Sony studio.

So we get to the hotel—it's just okay, nothing to write home about—and when the producers check in, the first thing we ask is: *Who's on the panel—which sharks?* And they tell us: Mark Cuban, Robert Herjavec, Mr. Wonderful, Daymond John, and Lori Greiner.

No Barbara.

The two of us don't need to discuss it. "No," I say, "we want Barbara."

"Listen, that's tomorrow's panel. It's your opportunity, so take it."

"Okay, well then, we're not gonna show up."

We don't say it in a rude way, I don't think we come off as entitled or arrogant. But we've got a plan, and we believe in ourselves, and we're sticking with our gut.

And knowing us by now as they do, they have a pretty good idea we're not bluffing.

An hour or so later, they call us back and they say, "Fine, you'll come on Wednesday night and we'll shoot on Thursday—Barb will be there then."

So on Wednesday we go back to the hotel, and this time it's definitely the final countdown.

And actually it gets a little weird. We start rehearsing as usual, standing in front of the mirror, going back and forth. "Hi, I'm Jim Tselikis and this is my cousin Sabin," and then Sabin takes over and does his sentence. But as this is happening, Sabin takes a pillow from the bed and smashes me in the face with it. So, okay, this is a new wrinkle, it's designed to throw me off, so I just keep talking. But now he takes a lamp, unplugs it, and wraps the cord around my neck. I swear, he's so into it, it's like I might be found dead in the hotel the next day—they'll call it "the Shark Tank murder"—but I'm still talking. And then, why not, I do the same to him. It's like the culmination of all the insane stuff we've been doing all these weeks.

Around six the next morning we get bussed to the studio—and for me it gets even more nerve-racking. Unlike Sabe, I've never been on a studio lot before, and it's not at all what I expect. It's nothing like the opening credits of a Warner Bros movie, with the music and the panoramic shots of the sound stages. The sound stages here look like a bunch of Home Depots, not welcoming at all. They all have signs attached, which you see after they pick you up, driving past in your golf cart: *Modern Family*, *The Goldbergs*, *The Queen Latifah Show*, and it's like "Oh, my God, when you watch and think it's happening on the street or in a bar, it's really happening right in *there*."

And, somehow, *this* starts making me nervous.

So then we roll up to the *Shark Tank* building, get off the golf cart, and they walk us inside. And suddenly there's the set we've been seeing on TV all this time, only it's different. The chairs and background are familiar, but everything is a façade—fake walls held up by two-by-fours, and on the side, doing their thing, are technicians and cameramen.

Then they walk you off to the green room to wait your turn.

They can't tell you for sure when that'll be—they try to get through ten or twelve groups each day, starting around seven in the morning and going to 6 or 7 PM—but they estimate roughly 10:30 or 11 AM.

Perfect! Shortly before the sharks break for lunch, they'll be famished. Our truck is parked out back, with people set to heat up both our Connecticut rolls and Maine rolls, more than enough for all of them.

Except we sit there and time's passing, and it's obviously moving slower than they expected, and there's no word when we'll be on. We fill the time rehearsing our lines, but it's not the same as before, because it's like we're racehorses primed to go, and nothing's happening. So the more we rehearse, the more I feel like I'm losing my edge, and I start worrying I'll go blank at the crucial moment.

Finally someone comes in and says we're pushed to 12 PM; and then we get pushed again to 12:30, and we're like *Fuck!* And now the guy comes in and it's, "Hey, the sharks are gonna break for lunch; you guys are up right after lunch."

It's a nightmare—they're gonna come back filled up on sandwiches or meatballs, and they're not gonna even want to *look* at food. Even if they love lobster, they'll have a bite and it won't look or taste nearly as good.

But it is what it is.

So right after lunch we're brought out past the big fake walls and placed behind these two big doors that viewers see open up. I've worn a cross since I was young and always rubbed before plane flights or hockey games, and I give it one last rub now. Then the doors open.

I give Sabe a little pound, and we walk down the hall. As the viewers are seeing me and Sabin for the first time, what we're seeing, forty feet ahead, is Mark Cuban and the other sharks, and the set, and a bunch of people with headsets on, and *Holy shit, it just got real!*

We stop where the producers told us to, at a little dot in the rug. And, I tell you, on TV it may look like the sharks are farther away, but they're actually right there on top of you.

So we're standing on the dot, and we're ready to start—right? But, no, what they do is try and freeze you and get you off your game by making you stand there for probably a minute and a half doing nothing. So we just stare back at Herjavec and Cuban and Barbara, smiling awkwardly, looking at the beautifully lit set, the rug, their table, their chairs, but behind them and off to the sides, it's just pitch black, though there are all those people and cameras in the darkness.

Then suddenly from the blackness someone yells "Go!" It's our signal to start into our pitch.

"Sharks, my name Sabin Lomac . . ."

". . . and I am his younger cousin Jim Tselikis . . ."

". . . And together we are Cousins Maine Lobster."

It goes off without a hitch, and we're rolling.

When our segment airs, like most others, it will run about ten or eleven minutes.* What viewers don't realize is that what they see is the product of rigorous editing. Because you're actually standing there in front of the sharks for more than an hour, and they whittle it down from there.

Still, the first minute and a half is key. That's when you want to establish credibility, both for your company or product and for yourselves. You want to show you have what it takes to bring the enterprise to the next level and beyond.

And unlike other shows, there are no second chances. If you screw up—if you falter, or are flustered, or say something stupid—there's no one to call "Cut" and let you start over. It's in there, and they'll probably use it.

But we totally nail that first minute and a half. And after that it becomes pretty much straight questions and answers about the business, which we've rehearsed the shit out of. I won't say it goes off perfectly. The fact is, only three months in, we *don't* have all the answers, at least not definitive ones. But we accomplish what we planned. We're calm, we're rational, we're confident. We know stuff but don't come across as egotistical or aggressive.

Part of the appeal of the show to viewers—and what makes it terrifying for some of those in the spotlight—is that it exposes people pretty fast. If you're no good on camera, or, worse, are crazy enough

* You can watch it here: https://www.youtube.com/watch?v=EQUuPQv9EHs.

to go on without knowing everything there is to know about your business, you're naked up there and totally vulnerable. You've got nationally known business giants shitting all over your business and basically saying you shouldn't even be here.

It's a sweatbox, and when the sharks start coming at you, it can really do a number on you psychologically. It's not personal; it's their job. And part of *your* job, when Mark Cuban looks at you in that way of his and asks about your financials, is to give as good as you get—or at least give *something* that passes as credible.

You also have to know how to navigate your way *between* the sharks, because at any moment they're apt to start going after one another. So at one point we're trying to answer Cuban, and Daymond interrupts with something totally different; so instead of getting flustered, Sabe starts politely answering Daymond; and then Cuban cuts in that he's asked us twice about our financials and isn't getting answers because we're dodging the question, so "I'm out!"

The truth, which we can only hope viewers see, is that we aren't avoiding his question at all—he just won't give us the ten seconds it takes to answer it. Because it's not like our answers are all that complicated. We've only been in business a few months and we're already profitable, doing around $100,000 in sales per month; and, who knows, if he listens maybe he'll love the sound of it and make an offer.

But, anyway, he's out.

So now Daymond tells us that we're asking too much for too small a piece of the company, and we are "halfway in a body bag." So he's also out; and Mr. Wonderful says he can't believe we're the only guys in Maine that can go out and get lobster, and he's also out.

But, of course, all along we're targeting Barbara, who up 'til now has been pretty quiet. But when Robert Herjavec makes an offer—twice the money, $100,000, but for 25% equity, instead of the 5%

we've proposed—she makes one too. She'll give the $55,000 we've requested, but for 17% of the company "because seventeen is my lucky number."

There's a moment of hesitation—if this was a sweatbox before, the heat is really on now—and I say, "Well, if you guys become part of the business, do you mind if I ask you what you might be able to do in assisting with growth?"

Which in retrospect is incredibly risky, because who the fuck am I? I'm a young kid, and we've been in business all of three months. And, sure enough, Herjavec's response boils down to: I don't need to answer to you. I'm sitting up here, you're down there.

But when Barbara answers, it's clear she's exactly who we've thought she was all these months, a total straight shooter. "Listen," she tells us, "let me get my hands on this business, and your faces and this brand are gonna be everywhere. I'm gonna do the marketing and the colors and all the rest."

I mean, wow, this is awesome!

So Sabin turns to me and says, "JT?"

I say back to Sabin: "Your call, Bro."

He claims that I blacked out at that moment, which at that point to some degree I probably did, and he says, "Barbara, welcome to the family."

Spontaneously, the three of us do a hug, with Barbara in the middle—what's come to be known as the infamous "lobster sandwich."

Sabin and I walk off, really excited, doing a high five on the way out. It's over. We negotiated Barbara's 17% offer down to 15%, and the deal is done.

Well, not quite.

Because instead of being taken outside, we're led back to the green room, where there's a *psychologist* waiting! What is this? But then you realize: Not everyone has a happy ending. Some people's heads are totally messed up by the experience. And the lawyers need to make sure the show is covered.

After we assure the guy we're in a good headspace, we walk from the vast studio building out into the blazing California afternoon. Back to normal life, back to reality, no celebrities around.

And, hey, suddenly it hits you. *Wait, what did we just do? Did we just give away 15% of our company—for $55,000?*

So, yeah, maybe the shrink made perfect sense, even for us.

I, at least, get over it fast. As we head back to Sabin's one-bedroom in West Hollywood, I'm thinking about who am I gonna call first. I gotta call my dad and my mom!

As soon as we get to his place, I sit under a tree in the shade and start dialing. My dad and mom are really happy for us, and very reassuring. My dad is extremely rational and levelheaded, and he tells me he gets it, all of this is new, and it's scary giving up 15%. But wasn't getting Barbara our goal? Why doubt ourselves now that we've achieved it? We should be embracing the likelihood of all the good things that will come our way because of her.

When I go inside, Sabin's in his bed—under the covers. He's called a few buddies and confidants from previous jobs, asking them all variations on the same questions: Why do we need her? What can she really do for our business? Won't she put it under? Fair enough questions, except he's not looking for answers, just confirmation of the nightmare scenario in his head that we've made the biggest mistake of our lives.

"Dude," I keep trying to reassure him, "this is good, this is an opportunity. Let's go to the bar and celebrate."

But he's not buying it. From under the covers, I hear him ask his buddy Mike if he thinks this is the end of Cousins Maine Lobster.

He's also wondering if we can get out of the deal.

"Dude," I say, "do you realize how few people get to do this? Go on *Shark Tank* and walk away with a deal? And it's exactly the one we wanted!"

But that's just Sabe. Having now been in this business together fourteen years, it is one of the things I accept: When we hit highs, whether it's opening new sites, hitting new income levels, winning awards, or going on *The Today Show*, he never really celebrates them. He never takes a moment to smell the roses before sprinting on to the next thing.

On this day—which will turn out to be by far the most important of our business lives—it'll be six or eight hours before he shakes it off. But when he does, he's immediately his old self. We end up late that night at Barney's Beanery, around the corner, drinking away all our concerns, and Sabin's the life of the party.

CHAPTER 8

Bringing Barbara Aboard

SABIN

It's true, I went home that day and stayed under the covers and was just completely down and negative.

Partly I'm sure it has to do with the fact that the process has been so stressful and intense, and now that it's over, it feels like a letdown. And even though we've gotten what we said we wanted, experience tells me something's off; there's got to be a catch.

I mean, that's just my mentality generally.

I know how crazy that sounds. Looking back, if we hadn't done *Shark Tank*, it's hard to imagine what the business would be today. Probably just a couple of trucks in Los Angeles.

Anyway, whatever concerns I have about Barbara disappear quite quickly.

After the show, we hear from someone on her team. They're doing their due diligence, to make sure the numbers we gave out aren't bullshit—that we're actually filing tax returns and I'm not in hock for a Lamborghini or owe my mom three hundred grand.

Shout out to Jim's dad!

Later I'll learn that a lot of deals that get done on the show don't come to fruition because they find out something's off.

Soon as that's done, we get word that *Shark Tank* wants to come up to Maine to shoot what they call a "home package"—a couple of minutes showing recent winners in their home environment that they use to tease the opening of the show. This is a big deal, and what's even better is that Barbara's gonna come up for it.

Not counting our exchanges on the air, I've only spoken to her one time, briefly, about a couple of details in the contract. So I hardly know the woman, and when we talk, after I learn she's planning to attend, I let her know there are some nice hotels in Portland and offer to give her assistant some recommendations. Hearing this, she doesn't immediately respond, so to be polite, I add, "Of course, you're also welcome to stay at my house."

"Okay," she says, "I'll do that."

All I can manage is: "Huh?"

"Yeah, I'll stay with you." Pause. "Do you mind if I bring my daughter?"

So that was the first taste of who she is, and how *different* from what you expect.

Two weeks later, there she is in my house, along with her seven-year-old daughter. And it is unreal how easygoing and unaffected and natural she is. I mean, when her daughter goes to bed, it's me and Barbara in our pajamas drinking white wine and playing Scrabble and shooting the shit.

She's someone completely without pretension. She's not polished at all, and unlike so many people who've worked their asses off to reach her level, she doesn't pretend to be. She curses a lot. She's just totally who she is, not a phony bone in her body.

Jimmy's parents are right down the road. I also own a second home there. Over the next few days the three of us discuss the business. She thinks we should add more trucks, says that from an investment standpoint, it's crazy not to. She also suggests we add "Fresh" to our name, changing it to Cousins Fresh Maine Lobster. We'll toy with this, and even get it trademarked—but decide it's too unwieldy, and of course never do.

But mainly she asks questions. About everything. So many that we're kind of like, *How do you not know this, you're Barbara Corcoran?* But how would she? She's not from Maine, she doesn't do lobster. So she asks.

That's a measure of her humility, but it's also a major business lesson: If you're unsure about something, screw appearances, keep asking until you get the answers.

It also immediately reinforces, if by now there's any doubt, that she's not interested in taking control. She lets us know she'll be as fully available as we want or need her to be; if we want to talk twice a month, that's what we'll do; if once a month is easier, we'll do that. And if something unexpected comes up and we need her input, we should shoot her a text and she'll get back to us right away.

But the company is our baby, and we're in charge.

In fact, in the early years, we'll talk to her a lot, about all kinds of things, some that might seem trivial or mundane but at the time felt momentous. Like, for instance, having to fire our first manager, who had become a friend.

Today, if necessary, I'll fire someone swiftly. But back then, I worried myself sick over it for months, until I finally talked to Barbara: *How do I do it? What do I say?*

Thinking back, these are obviously pretty dumb questions for someone running a business to have to ask anyone, especially someone like Barbara. But she got it, she's been there, and she knows how complicated the interpersonal part can be. It's not heartless to fire someone, she tells me, it's responsible, because it's protecting the business and everyone involved in it.

There are dozens of things like that. It's not that the advice was necessarily groundbreaking or revolutionary, but it helped us start building the confidence that would be essential to our long-term success.

I mean, at this point we're not only unsure of ourselves as businessmen, we're still trying to figure out who we are as *people.* Here we've had this massive overnight success, so how am I even supposed to *be* now? Do I need to be clean shaven and start wearing a suit and tie? Can I still curse as much?

What she taught us—almost inadvertently, by example—is that being yourself really is the secret sauce. I know it's a cliché, but for me it's still a total revelation, like a lightbulb in my consciousness: *Jesus, if Barbara Corcoran can act like this and still be successful, then we sure as shit can do it too!*

At this point, we've known Barbara for fourteen years, and with the company now running as smoothly as it is, and most of the earlier challenges met, we don't talk as regularly as we used to. Now it's even more of a personal relationship. When I come to New York, I'll still stay at her house, and we'll still shoot the shit. But these days, questions I'll ask will be less about business and more about kids and life.

BARBARA CORCORAN

Since we on *Shark Tank* know nothing about the potential entrepreneurs until they are on the stage, we meet them and form an impression at the same time as the audience. And my first impression of Sabin and Jim was *God, are they handsome! I wouldn't mind looking at them all the time!* It's not that I'm horny, but I always appreciate good looks. I think they have a lot to do with success, especially in the sales game.

So that was the first thing. But then they came in with a phenomenal pitch. It clearly communicated their vision, who they were going to be and how they were going to get there. Their preparation was top tier, and it showed.

I wasn't surprised when I learned later that they'd watched every episode of *Shark Tank* before they came on, which no one else had ever done, or that they'd gamed every possible argument and every possible question from every shark with three-by-five cards and drilled each other on the answers.

I loved that they talked about taking a personality test. That was something else I'd never seen before. They weren't afraid to find out where their weaknesses were, and how, even though they'd known each other their whole lives, they wanted to know how they'd run the business together.

And, boy, were they quick-witted. They'd take a question and immediately pivot to turn it their way to make a point they wanted to make. Street smart—which I put tremendous value on, as opposed to book smart, which chases me away. All my great entrepreneurs are street smart.

Plus, these guys were wildly enthusiastic about the company and where it was going. You'd think that's something every young entrepreneur would be—right? But you'd be surprised how many come in without that kind of energy or self-belief. And I'm always on the lookout for that, because the classic pattern is that about three months after *Shark Tank*, nothing goes according to plan. Something happens that craps on the business—the market goes bad, or there's bad blood with a supplier, or interest rates go to hell—and they're not up to the challenge. And as soon as I hear someone behaving like a victim instead of fighting back, I'm done, that's all I need to know.

It's a big reason I never invest in rich kids. When there are rich kids on the set, I always ask the question *Where did you get your money from?* Because the minute they say "family and friends," I know it's from dad. And I also know dad will give them some more if things don't go well, and that takes the hunger away. You know, there's something beautiful about a kid that's never had a good vacation or had a nice car, or never had time off or saw a beachfront or whatever else riches bring, and they have to earn it for themselves. That need drives them.

I remember when I opened the Corcoran Group, on day one I could already taste what it would become, and that I was gonna be the queen of real estate. It was based on absolutely nothing, but I could see it in my mind's eye. I knew what clothes I would wear. I knew how people would kiss my ring just like the pope. It was realer than real, because I *needed* to make it happen.

And I saw that need in these two. They weren't going to let it fail, and they had the toughness to make sure that didn't happen. They would get past the obstacles because their mentality wasn't a blamer or victim mentality. They'd take on the responsibility of overcoming the obstacles, and keep going.

Of course, mainly this was a gut reaction, because it was before I knew anything more about either of them—and Sabin would turn out to be a much more classic example of that neediness than Jim, who had a much more solid upbringing. But I could already see that fierce drive to succeed in both.

Sabin was the consummate salesman and closer, he could talk a dog off a meat wagon. You'd buy anything from him. And Jim, though he's more analytical—where Sabin is up in the air dreaming half the time—always has his feet on the ground and is also a great salesman. Which is great, because you can't ever have enough salesmanship in a partnership.

How good a pair of salesmen were they? They were so convincing and solid that when they described how phenomenally well the company was doing—"$150,000 this month, the highest month ever"—not one of us thought to ask the question that we *always* ask: "How long have you been in business?" Because the answer was that it was only the *one* month!

When I heard the numbers, I assumed it was for at least a year, because of the way they phrased it, in terms of monthly numbers. And my thinking was *Oh my God, if that one unit's this profitable, I could build a franchise!* Because you already had the bones of a franchise, and I saw right away I could help to grow the business because I think that's where my strength is.

The truth is, I'd have felt that way even if I'd had the full story. In fact, maybe even more so, because that's how persuasive they were. Because I already knew I'd be getting two terrific entrepreneurs for the price of one, and two guys that would build a strong team and not tolerate losers around them.

So pretty much from the minute I saw them, I knew if I could get them for the right price I'd make an offer. I just had to keep my mouth shut so no one saw I was drooling.

I had no idea at the time they'd been targeting me all along. They made strong eye contact with every shark—looked us all straight in the eye and answered the questions. They were straight shooters and straight shooters treat people equally. If I knew they had wanted me so badly, I would have offered them less.

I haven't even talked about the whole family element they were creating in the company. It's not something easily done in a business, but when it's truly an objective, and you achieve it, it can be incredibly important in reaching your goals.

I knew how much they meant it when they opened their arms and Sabin said, "Welcome to the family." Maybe I just imagined it, but I think I saw a little tear in his eye.

JIM

Barb—She's One of a Kind

It is three months since our *Shark Tank* deal, and I realize there's no putting off taking the final, fatal step. Sitting in a quiet corner of the Panera Bread outlet near my office, I carefully compose the letter to my bosses telling them I'm quitting my job.

But even as I write I'm still having second and third thoughts. *What the hell am I doing? I'm twenty-five years old and have this really, really good career, making $100,000 to $120,000 in commissions. All my friends are around, and I get to go to Bruins games with them whenever I want, and my parents are just two hours north. And I'm leaving all this to do a food truck on the other side of the country?! Without any idea what kind of revenue it'll produce long term? And, by the way, having to split it with another guy?*

Up 'til now, I've told myself that maybe I could manage to do both things simultaneously; that maybe the food truck would be just a side thing. It'd be a great way to represent Maine and our family, and also generate some extra income, while I stayed in Boston, and both of us would keep our regular jobs.

Pretty implausible, I know. Still, as long as there was no firm guarantee our *Shark Tank* episode would ever even air—since they shoot around eighty groups a season, but only have room for sixty-five—it was at least a possibility.

Only no more. We've now gotten the *Great-news-you've-got-an-air-date!* email from the show, followed by word that a crew (and Barbara) will be coming to Maine to shoot a "home package" introducing our segment. And with millions of people about to see us on TV, the chances of my owners and managers, and the doctors and nurses I work with, not hearing about it are pretty remote. And what would I tell them? *Yes, I was on the show, but it's my cousin's company, I just invested in it?*

It's obviously long past time to figure out my shit.

I've given the letter a lot of thought, and I write it with great care. It is honest and deeply respectful, saying how much I've enjoyed the work and expressing gratitude for the opportunity they've given me. But I also remind them what their own bosses told them when they were young and about to leave their jobs in corporate America to start their own small company: *Hey, if it doesn't work out, you're always welcome back.*

And they take it as I hoped. They wish me luck, and they say that if I ever need to come back, the door will always be open.

But of course—as I'd realized that morning after I pressed "Send"—now there really is no turning back.

Nowadays, with the show being the huge success it is and their time at a premium, it's rare for the sharks to go to some out-of-the-way Podunk place to visit a bagel business or ice cream shop they've invested in. But back then, Season Four, they were all still interested in promoting the show—and even then, Barbara was by far the most hands-on of them all.

My first impression of her? It was twofold. Part A: I've never met anyone in the public eye so genuine. She doesn't do a shtick like Mr. Wonderful, playing a character on TV. She's kind and authentically likes people, and she especially admires those with grit and ambition. What you see is what you get.

Part B: How to put this? I've also never met anyone so completely and totally uninhibited. She's a total free spirit, with no filter, always says exactly what she wants to in the way she wants to say it, without hesitation or embarrassment.

At the beginning, it can be kind of shocking.

I mean, she's staying up the road at Sabin's in Scarborough, at a little rental property he has there, and one evening my parents invite her to their place for dinner. So we're having a bunch of wine, us, my mom and dad, and my sister, and Barbara asks, "Hey!"—speaking to my mom and dad—"Steve and Julie, when's the last time you had sex?"

I'm like, *Whoa, who is this lady?* and *Oh, wait, she's kidding.* But, no, she's not kidding, and that's who she is—a total straight shooter for whom no subject is off-limits—and she asks because she's genuinely interested. Maybe it's because she's a little bit older, and she has nothing to lose, but she just doesn't give a fuck, and whether it's sex or politics or anything else, she just speaks her mind.

But Sabe and I love it. Because for guys like us, it makes her completely relatable. I mean, it's hard to imagine hanging out with Mark Cuban, but with Barbara, it immediately feels like she's a buddy. There's never that air of celebrity, or *I've got a ton of money and you don't.*

I'll never forget the first time she met Sabe's buddy Shaun. He'd just joined the company, and he'd been sweating bullets because we were all going to dinner together and he was so nervous to meet her.

So Shaun shows up in a suit and a tie, and the first thing she says to him is, "Hey, Shaun, what do you do, what's your role?" and he tells her he's gonna be involved in the franchising. She looks at him, smiles, and says, "Okay, good. Just don't fuck it up, 'cause if you do, I'm gonna chop your balls off."

Talk about an icebreaker! Immediately they're completely on the same page, and they spend the rest of the evening kidding around back and forth.

We like to say how great it would be if they ever did a reality show of *Shark Tank: Behind the Curtain*, 'cause Barbara would be such a revelation. This is what she looks like without makeup, this is what she's like in pajamas, this is what she says when no one's expecting it.

CHAPTER 9

First Hurdle

LOVE YOU, MOM!

SABIN

Our segment is slotted for October 12, so we decide to pull out all the stops and do a big watch party in Maine. We rent a big conference room at a hotel in Portland and invite one hundred people—parents, friends, cousins, of course, and also lobster vendors and lobstermen. So the place is packed, and we're paying for it with money we don't have.

As broadcast time draws near, the atmosphere is both celebratory and a little anxious, because aside from our parents, no one else in the room knows for certain what's coming.

The show begins with the opening package showing Maine, and people are loving it, because how often do you see Maine featured on national television? And now they're giving the picture-postcard version, with the lobster shack, the lighthouse, the fog over the water.

Then we see me and Jim, and people start whistling and cheering. And from there it transitions to the actual show, as we're walking into the *Shark Tank* in our beachcomber outfits. And, bang, we're into our opening, describing the company and its early success to the sharks.

But soon enough, Mr. Wonderful starts ripping on us—calling us "greedy crustaceans" and asking if we really think we're the only ones from Maine who can do this. People start booing, and the boos get even louder a moment later when Cuban snaps "Okay, guys, I'm out!"

Everyone's engaged and having fun, and in the middle of all this we're getting texts from Barbara, who's also seeing the finished product for the first time, telling us we look great, and sound great, and that this is just a fantastic representation of the business.

In the room by now there's probably a little more apprehension over whether we'll get a deal at all—though, of course, why would we be throwing a party if we hadn't? Still, they're living this for the first time, in what feels like real time, and who knows how things work in television?

Meanwhile, as the minutes tick by we're getting more on edge also. Because a key part of the presentation we made to the sharks back in July has not yet been heard by the eight to nine million people watching tonight: that, yes, we have a food truck, but guess what? We've also got an e-commerce business. So if you want our food—crab cakes, lobster cakes, chowder, bisque, lobster mac and cheese, lobster pot pies, whatever—we'll ship it directly to your door the next day.

Though it began as a way of countering expected criticism by the sharks of our original truck-only model, we've convinced ourselves it should be an essential part of the business, since it allows us to immediately go nationwide. Moreover, we've talked to other online businesses that have been on *Shark Tank* about the show's impact, like Daisy Cakes, and once Barbara is on board, we've asked her too.

And the answer is consistent: the so-called *Shark Tank* effect is real. People do multiple hundreds of thousand dollars in additional sales, sometimes a million, in the days following an appearance on the show. You just have to be ready, and make sure your website doesn't crash.

So we've spent the last three months adding a slick e-commerce component to our website, and on this very night, we're set up to accept orders and ship product. We have $250,000 of frozen inventory ready to go out the door, with people poised by computers to take orders that we figure should add up to between $500,000 to $600,000 in sales.

But we have no idea how the tape has been edited.

And now we watch as Barbara gives us our deal, and Sabin says "Welcome to the family," and the three of us do the Cousins Lobster sandwich, and in Portland everyone cheers and applauds because they're so excited and relieved.

And we sit there dumbstruck. It's a disaster!

How could it happen? We described the e-commerce thing to the sharks *at length.* How could every second of that wind up on the cutting room floor?!

The woman we've hired to run our e-commerce is there, staring at a computer. I go over to her and ask, "How are we doing? How many orders have come through?"

I'm prepared for the worst; I'm expecting to hear eighty, or maybe a hundred.

"We're at nine," she says.

Yes, nine. And those were all from family. Thanks, Aunt Betsy, but this is bad.

The rest of the night is a blur. When we go out with our whole family, Jimmy and I get trashed, absolutely hammered. The next morning, we wake up with hellacious hangovers, and we go down to our offices to see just how bad things are. We're up to fourteen orders.

So we've gone from an epic high—the buildup, the airing, everyone's excitement as it unfolds—to this epic low.

I mean, we're truly looking into the abyss. It's like, *Okay, we're just gonna to have to run the truck for another year and a half to pay this off. After that, we're done.*

Enter the little angel on our shoulder named Barbara Corcoran.

When we talk to her, it's like in her mind this is the tiniest bump in the road. It's all positive energy and good vibes. She assures us the episode was fantastic, we're launched, we're on our way—we're going to be the quickest success the show's ever had. She tells us the best entrepreneurs are the ones who don't feel sorry for themselves but get up quick and figure it the fuck out, and that's what we'll do.

Over the years people have actually asked us why we'd give away a big chunk of our business for only $55,000? They say they've got an uncle or a friend who'd have given us a lot more than that for just a few points.

That's the difference between an investor and a partner. And, in our case, between the business amateurs we were and a partner like Barbara.

Let's put it this way: Two weeks later, she gets us on a *Good Morning America* segment called "Steals and Deals," where they feature all kinds of stuff at reduced prices. The host announces: "Here, from Cousins Maine Lobster, we have lobster mac and cheese." She scoops some up, takes a bite, and, exclaims, "Oh, my God, it's SO good!"

I'm back east, watching this live, but Jim's in my place in Los Angeles where it's four in the morning, so he won't see it for another three hours. But he has the whole back-end system for the website up and he's just watching the orders just fly in. In a few hours we do $275,000 in sales, and the whole inventory problem is taken care of.

All Barbara. She straight-up gives us a Get Out of Jail card.

JIM

The Girl

I make the move to LA the week after the broadcast—though since I don't yet have a place of my own, at first it's back to sleeping on Sabin's air mattress. This isn't great, sharing the one bathroom, tiptoeing around each other and moving the damn air mattress every day, but since I'm working my face off 24/7, there's no time to find an apartment.

And when I do, it's pretty sobering. I mean, in Boston I was splitting rent on a place with a couple of buddies. But now, renting my own place, right off the bat I'm on the hook for twice what I was paying then—and that's on top of having to ship my car and all my stuff across the country. And with no salary or commissions, every damn thing's coming out of my savings.

True, the truck continues to draw spectacularly. As we proudly told the world on *Shark Tank*, we're doing $100,000 a month in sales. Which *sounds* great. Everyone thinks we're big-time entrepreneurs and just rolling in it.

But the truth is, between our inexperience and outright stupidity, our *profits* are nowhere what they should be. For one thing, our UPS bill is through the roof, because we're shipping overnight not only our fresh lobster meat—which of course is essential—but also pallets of frozen soups that can just as easily go on a truck and get to us in four days.

Meanwhile, at $13 we're *under*pricing our rolls. How come? We think the lower price point is the key to bringing in customers. In fact, as we will learn, most people are not just willing to pay a little more for quality, they intuitively grasp that they *need* to. I mean, I love sushi, but if I go to a place and they're selling a tuna roll for $3.50, my first question is *What the fuck's wrong with this?* I'm probably not even gonna eat it. But if you tell me a tuna roll's nine or ten bucks, I figure I'm in for something special.

In retrospect this is all obvious, but we have a steep learning curve.

So, yeah, we have $100,000 in monthly sales. But we end up clearing maybe $15,000 in profit, and that's split between two guys.

When I come home for Christmas, my father, who we've asked to run the books, lays down the law. He details exactly what we earned in the month of November and so far in December and says: You're not taking this money. You can take two or three thousand, but you can't take $7,500. You have to leave the rest in the bank, because you have to grow the reserves to make sure you cover our vendors in Maine, or to deal with problems that come up with the truck, and all the other rainy-day expenses sure to arise.

Anyway, by the time everything's accounted for, big-time entrepreneurs and celebrities that we are, we're making about $3,000 each—around $36,000 a year! A little more than a quarter of what I was making at Stryker.

If things continue like this, pretty soon I won't even be able to afford my own groceries.

So he talks to me about how we might fine-tune the operation to make it more profitable, by doing more sales or cutting expenses, or both.

Well, the most obvious way is put a second truck on the road, then maybe a third and fourth, which will theoretically quadruple profits, and over the course of the year, get me back to Stryker money, and potentially beyond.

Of course, this is so obvious that even we have thought of it. The problem is that, with only one truck, we're working our asses off to the point of exhaustion, so we've put off the idea.

But now we're facing the reality that one truck won't work for two guys. And the truth is, we've chosen to ditch our old lives and do what we're doing not just to make more money but also because we wanted to challenge ourselves in major ways. And this is the way to freaking do it!

So, yeah, we'll do another truck, and maybe another after that. And we'll work even harder to make it work, as hard as we have to, to the exclusion of everything else.

Well, no, not exactly *everything*, at least not in my case. Because there's this girl . . .

I actually met her while I was still on the job with Stryker back east. I'm at the Lahey Clinic in Burlington, outside Boston, and I see this really beautiful blonde girl. Except she's also a medical device rep, and we're both masked up, so all I really see are her eyes and hair. We might as well be in full hazmat suits.

Since it's a work situation, we don't get to talk, but afterward I see her full face, and as she's about to get in her car and we go our separate ways, we chat a bit. So at least I know her name. Maggie.

I really don't know anything else about her but figure I know enough to follow up. Only when I try to find her, I run into a wall. Can't find her on Facebook, can't find her on LinkedIn, can't find her in any of the hospitals.

Then suddenly one day I see her walking down the hall, directly at me, and we make eye contact. But there's not even a flicker of recognition from her, which is really crushing. It's like *Wow, I really must not be memorable.*

A couple of weeks later, I see her again, and I call her on it. And what comes out of that is that the very day we first spoke and exchanged names, afterward she went for a run and got hit by a car. She was in the hospital for five days, and she still has staples in her head, and she doesn't remember anything from that day or from many of the days in between.

So we're putting the pieces together, and laughing about it, and at the same time starting from scratch. And I'm realizing I really, *really* like this girl.

But I know—though I can't tell anyone, because our segment hasn't been broadcast yet and I'm pledged to secrecy 'til then—that I'll probably be moving to California. And what kind of guy would I be if I started a relationship with a girl and didn't tell her that? So I try hard to keep it more or less on a friendship basis.

Though finally I do violate my rule, and I ask if she'd like to grab a beer. Immediately she blushes, I mean gets really red, which I take as a sign that she likes me too. But she says no, there's really no point—because *she'll* be moving to California in a couple of months. She explains that her mother and stepfather live in San Diego, and she's decided to try medical device sales out there for a while to see if she prefers it to Boston.

Talk about a surprise—and really good news! On the other hand, how creepy is it gonna sound if I come back with: *Hey, I'm also going to Southern California*?

And even if I did, how would I explain that it's because I'm quitting my fantastic job to run a food truck?

Or that I'll hardly have time to breathe out there, let alone spend time with her, because for the foreseeable future my entire focus will be on building the company?

How's all *that* gonna fly?

So if this is a love story—and I'm hoping it will be—it'll come with a bunch of limits and complications that I know most women wouldn't put up with for a few weeks, let alone years.

CHAPTER 10

The Start of an Empire

SABIN

Right out of the gate Barbara's been telling us the same thing, that we should get another truck. She's like: *This is a cute little thing you got going here, but how am I gonna make my money back with one truck and not have it take forever? And by the way, Los Angeles is over five hundred square miles, with ten million people living in it.*

Would going from one to two—or three, and on from there—be an insane amount of work? Damn right. But fuck it, we're young and healthy; it's just a matter of focus and effort.

It's not like we're starting from zero; we already have a highly effective working model. And what started as a casual division of responsibilities—with Jimmy mainly handling bookings and promotion and me overseeing the trucks and overall operations—has been working perfectly, playing to our respective strengths.

And we make it happen. Cousins Maine Lobster will go from one truck to two in three months; and by early 2014, we'll have a total of four.

Sure enough, it takes all we have to give and then some—twelve and fourteen-hour days are the norm—and it also takes money. We're still buying used trucks, but even those go for upward of $90,000, before the costs of refurbishing and getting them road ready. But though business is booming, credit isn't easy to come by for a pair of newbies involved in a venture lenders don't necessarily understand.

We do have Barbara's $55,000 investment in our pocket, good enough for a down payment on the second truck. But we've made a promise to ourselves to save it for a rainy day. (It'll end up being a few years before we use it.)

The upshot is that even as we're trying to follow Steve's advice to pay down the existing debt from our profits, we have to squeeze out even more to keep moving forward. It strains our resources almost to the breaking point, and our nerves, but we cut enough corners to make it happen.

We get the work done on the trucks at a place in South LA, and it's not even close to the quality we do now. Every day Jim and I have to drop all our other work to be there, physically present and breathing in the seagull shit and the gross gray water, to first of all make sure the contractors are showing up, and then to make sure they're doing it right. It's almost like building a home—it's bare bones, then there's framing, and plumbing, and electrical.

I mean, if you think of a UPS truck or one of those linen-service trucks, they're basically just a box that opens up in the back. So the builder and his guys literally take this box and start cutting. They cut the huge window that will end up being under the awnings of our truck—since then, it's become two windows under two awnings. Then they cut around the wheels and increase the ceiling heights to do the cooking; they create space for the fridge, freezers, lowboys, and countertops; they put in the hood, the ventilation, the electric. Though at the time we don't yet have cameras on our trucks or a lot of tech, we still have wires running everywhere, from connecting various units.

This is before we understand that if we start with a better box we can majorly decrease both labor and expense. But back then it's custom work that we're doing on the cheap, with Jim and me driving down every day to South Central, saying *Can you move this here, and maybe put this there?* Which, since neither of us is an electrician or a plumber, takes a certain amount of guesswork and luck and balls.

And then comes the finishing touch—the paint job. Even then we're beginning to experiment with the look. On the second truck, we do a wrap that's a little shinier. Then, on the third truck, we do one that's more matte black; only afterward, we realize that when people touch the trucks as they're eating, the oil and butter on their fingers leaves marks that won't come off.

Then we try doing one with just decals and logos of the lobster and *Shark Tank*, so that it'll be less expensive to replace the logos than having to rewrap the entire truck. So we go through multiple variations to see which ones will adhere best, and then six or nine months later they're peeling off or they're fading in the sun because we used the cheaper shit.

The upshot is, in a lot of ways we still don't know what the hell we're doing. But we're working really, really, *really* hard, and trying to be as prepared as humanly possible in every way we can think of, and it's paying off.

The trucks may be pretty basic, and they're not entirely uniform. But they get the job done, and by the end of year two we're in four places at once, and selling a helluva lot more lobster rolls.

JIM

Without Sales, You Have No Business

With the new trucks, I'm totally working my ass off, setting up the bookings. They're on the road six days a week—every day but Monday, which is set aside for truck maintenance and rest—and I've got to find locations for each truck for three lunches and three dinners per week, plus three events on the weekends.

But like doing sales back at Stryker, it really gets my blood going.

Since I'm still fairly new to LA, and it's such a big place, I'm learning the town on the fly. I mean, if it's Portland, Maine, or

Boston, right off the bat I'll know there's a gas station on such and such a corner, with some high-end offices nearby and a ton of street traffic and the gas station has extra parking, as long as we don't get in the way of people coming in for gas. But LA's largely a blank slate, so a lot of it is driving around, learning the freeways and the streets, figuring out which places have possibilities, and then determining who we partner with.

A grocery store with a nice parking lot? An electronics store with good street traffic? A public space close to some office buildings—and, if so, how can we access the thousands of people inside them? Can I get someone in that high rise to blast out a mailer to all the people sitting at their desks saying, *Hey, Cousins Maine Lobster's going to be here tomorrow for lunch*?

Making and sustaining contacts is key, whether it's the assistant to the main guy or maybe the person at the front desk. Whoever I can find internally to spread the word that our truck is coming, and it'll not just be a huge upgrade over the brown-bag lunch or Subway sandwich you have every other day, it'll be an EVENT.

Even though we've parked in front of one building, there's five other buildings within walking distance we can draw from, so I'll also try to make contacts there—who I'll ask to put up flyers and send out an email blast. And most of the time, there's someone perfectly willing. It's not like fresh lobster is the hardest sell in the world, but you have to think, strategize, be creative, and put in the effort to award the results.

I also key in on weekend events—strawberry or apple festivals, civic events, public music festivals—as well as those likely to draw lobster fans. For instance, we like to do dog events, where they have them running through hoops and over courses. In LA they do dog events to a totally insane level, and people that spend money on their dogs will damn well also spend it on lobster.

It gets easier as time goes on. A lot of people who've never seen us have now heard about us, and what they've heard is always positive. And since our trucks are so distinctive, with our phone number prominently displayed on their sides, we're getting calls from people who've spotted us on the 405 or the 105, or any of a hundred city streets, suggesting places in their neighborhood where we might do business. In fact, everyone I meet seems to have ideas about where else we should go. I have dozens of business cards in my pocket, and emails on slips of paper, and I follow up on every one of them.

The Beverly Hills Art Show was not easy to crack. It's huge, draws a hundred thousand people over the course of the weekend, and brings in vendors from all over town. The hitch is they only allow six food trucks on the premises, and they already have a lobster truck.

I reach out and make my pitch anyway, urging them to at least give us a shot. No good, they turn me down. But I stay on the event coordinator's radar, keep emailing him every quarter 'til, guess what? The other lobster truck messes up. So he gives us a chance, lets us go *mano a mano* with the other truck; we get Saturday, they get Sunday. And after the coordinator sees how many more people we have in line, we end up getting both days.

Same thing happened at the Santa Anita racetrack. Big crowds, obviously lots of money to spend. While they gamble, they also have to eat, so they have food trucks on the infield. And, again, the other lobster truck is there; and, again, for the first year and a half the woman in charge won't give me the time of day.

So one afternoon what I do is bring the truck outside Santa Anita, bring some rolls up to the office, knock on the door, and introduce myself. I tell them I know the other truck is already here, all I ask is that you try our food. That's all it takes—she notices a difference immediately, and instead of giving us different days, she puts us both there together, side by side, and lets the customers make the choice.

Result: All day we have forty or fifty people waiting in line and they have four or five.

So that's our mentality: Just try our food. Do that and in the future you won't go to anyone else.

And when eventually we have to start increasing prices because lobster prices have gone up, it doesn't make any difference, because they know what they're getting. Now they understand implicitly that a quality lobster roll *should* cost more than a chicken sandwich.

I also make sure we don't go to the same spot too often. Not because there aren't enough customers, but because I don't want to lessen the "event" factor. We're not talking burgers or pizza or tacos: There's a mystique attached to the product that's priceless, and I never want that to grow stale. It's why people will jump in their cars when they hear we're a half hour or even an hour away. People hear lobster—especially *Maine* lobster—and there are all kinds of instant associations. Over and over I hear, "Lobster, holy shit, I had that when I went to Maine," or "Hey, I went to Boston University!" We have a product people can actually get excited about.

And we enhance that with the quality of our service. We can make a bun and put together a lobster roll and get it out the window in thirty seconds, forty-five max, so even if we've got a line of eighty people, they're constantly moving, not standing there shuffling their feet; they see people are getting served. Meanwhile they're looking at the grilled cheese truck that also has a long line, only after fifteen minutes the person who was twenty people back is still seventeen people back, because in the damn truck they've got to cook through the damn cheese.

Geniuses that we are, before we started it didn't even occur to us that having such a quick speed of ticket would be such a gigantic plus. But once we saw it, we built on it by hiring staff members who have what it takes to get stuff out the window *really* fast.

Just like there are certain people who can shuck oysters in split seconds, there are those gifted at measuring the exact right amount of lobster meat, placing it in the roll, and *boom*, moving it out the window—and doing it without getting butter all over the wax paper. Because we also pride ourselves on presentation. This is a gourmet product, and everything must look like it's been done with method and meaning.

People who don't have those skills might move to a different station, or be trained up, or sometimes they just won't make it. There's no room for compromise with efficiency. As in most things, it usually won't take long to see if someone will work out. They either get it and show promise or they don't.

Incidentally, something else we hear, and pretty often, is *Hey, I had this exact same idea as you guys two or three or five years ago*—to which we'll nod, and smile, and not say the obvious.

The difference is: We did it.

CHAPTER 11

What's Franchising?

SABIN

What we hadn't counted on was that our early success came with a big potential downside. We started to think we were bulletproof.

Which set us up for a hard dose of reality.

I should probably say up front, if only in self-defense, that the notion of going brick and mortar wasn't our idea. We're approached by the owner of a place that was already in business, a lounge of some sort. The owner tells us it's doing great, really busy, and that he needs to serve food to have a liquor license. He's heard a lot about Cousins Maine Lobster and the lines of people waiting for our food, and since he wants quality, not the usual bar menu, he thinks it'll be a perfect marriage.

My immediate reaction? "Definitely! Holy shit, *a real restaurant!*"

Of course, it's all ego, because, let's face it, there's a bit of an inferiority thing involved with running food trucks. Not only are they unsexy, they don't feel as solid or respectable as a regular restaurant.

So we check it out, and talk some more with the guy, and with our general manager, and though I don't know my ass from my elbow, in my mind it's looking better and better. In fact, I'm thinking this is a real opportunity. It could be a stepping stone for potentially transforming our entire model to brick and mortar, a means of testing the market.

True, Barbara strongly counsels us against it, urging us to stick to our own lane. But what does she know, she's only a hugely successful entrepreneur! What could possibly go wrong with opening this restaurant in the middle of some guy's nightclub?

And it's not like we're the only ones who love the idea. The weekend we open, our old friends at UrbanDaddy blast out an item alerting Angelenos, "Next time you absolutely need some non-mobile lobster, you can go inside, head to the counter and order a pile of lobster-y goodness without going through the whole rigmarole of chasing the truck down on Twitter."

But it's a mistake. And soon it'll be a shitstorm.

Because it's not really our restaurant. The owner and his partner continue to run their club and we're just the food component. We're basically subletting a restaurant that doesn't match our brand, vibe, or company ethos. It's actually the opposite of everything we would do if given the chance to open a real restaurant.

I mean, this isn't one of those places in West Hollywood where Brad Pitt might walk through the door. It's more like a nightclub in Miami—except it's not Miami, it's on Colorado Boulevard in Pasadena. And even though the owner has had previous success with his own concept, it's not OUR concept. Huge miss.

Pretty soon we're seeing reviews from people who've been fans of Cousins Maine Lobster, wondering *What the hell's going on?* On weekends, there's actually a bouncer, and there needs to be, because there are lines out the door of people looking to get hammered.

So if you're some middle-aged couple who's shown up looking for a lobster roll, there's this hefty guy outside checking you out, asking for ID to prove you're twenty-one; and when you step inside there's dim lighting and you're looking at a wall with eighty bottles of booze, and people sitting on velvet couches sipping cocktails. You don't know what's going on, and you're right to wonder.

And on our end, it's like: *What in the world are we doing?* And the answer is: *No fucking clue.*

On top of which, we've negotiated a poor contract, which takes tons of money and energy to get out of. And the whole time it's just exhausting, because this is the same time we're getting the other trucks on the road and we are just spread too thin. Why did we do this? Ego.

At least, getting out when we do, the financial hit is also a lot less than it might have been.

Still, the cost was also in the time we wasted at this location, and in other opportunities missed. Because for guys like us, built to hustle 24/7 after new opportunities, time may be the most precious resource of all.

The biggest takeaway, or what should have been, is that given half a chance, we can mess up as colossally as anyone.

This whole time, while we're focusing on Los Angeles in both smart ways and dumb ones, Barbara's thinking a lot bigger.

As in: Why stop with LA? Why not just rinse and repeat, and do this thing *everywhere*?

Incredible as it seems, this is something that's never occurred to either me or Jim. I mean, looking back, what kind of dummies were we to not realize that if something like this works in one city, it might work in others? Even here in California, there's dozens of other potential locales.

Yet when Barbara first brings up the idea of franchising, my response is, "What's franchising?"

I'm not being a wiseass—I literally don't know what it means. I mean, I never went to business school, I've never had any interest in this kind of shit; all we're thinking about at this point is maybe getting another truck.

"Look," she tells me, "you could do this practically anywhere. There's no reason why you couldn't put this on the moon."

When I still don't get it, she explains the concept of franchising. Once we start franchising, she tells me, we could realistically expect the business to grow—and we need that, badly. With the initial fees and royalties from franchisees, we'd be able to take our brand across the country, plus we'd be setting up an entire training and education experience for our franchise partners. When she's telling me about how McDonald's and KFC did it, that's something I can understand.

Still, it takes a little while for us to get our heads around it. Could someone else in another city be successful with this concept? Could multiple others, in multiple cities? Could we assume that kind of managerial role, where we'd provide the product and the training and supervision at a distance?

It's a tremendous mental leap, to be sure, but we slowly come around to Barbara's idea that franchising is the company's future. Yes, it's uncharted territory, but on the plus side, the possibilities are limitless—and why else are we doing this, if not to shoot for the moon?

Once we've fully talked it through, and made the decision, the first thing we do is call for reinforcements.

SHAUN HIGGINS

Basically, what happens is that two guys who know nothing about franchising call another guy who knows nothing about franchising to start up this department.

At the time, I'm in professional soccer, a player-coach with a team on Long Island called the Rough Riders, and I know close to zero about *any* aspect of the food truck or the lobster business. But now Sabin's on the phone, saying I should come out west to oversee franchising.

We met through sports. I went to Hofstra on a soccer scholarship, and we're close friends, really *best* friends, right from the get-go. I'm one of three boys, and in our family Sabin's the fourth brother.

So naturally I've been closely following Cousins Maine Lobster almost from the beginning.

I say "almost" because this is the one thing Sabin ever kept so close to his heart. He didn't say a word about it until about two weeks before they actually launched the first truck. It's because it was a passion project, and he didn't want other people to pour cold water on it, I guess, or to react the way that I did, which wasn't really so much negative as confused. I was like, *A food truck? Are you Mr. Softee? Are you the guy selling hot dogs by Madison Square Garden?* My other impression was that it was some kind of side gig.

But then it very quickly gets real. On the day they launch, literally before they sell a single roll, I get a call from Sabin, and he's incredibly excited: *Dude, we haven't even opened and there's already eighty people outside! This is going to be huge—do you wanna be a part of it?!* And I'm like, *I don't know, man—good luck, call me later.*

From that point forward I'm getting the play-by-play every step of the way: the email from *Shark Tank*; the back-and-forth on whether they should do it; their crazy prep for the show; Sabe freaking out after the taping, calling from under the sheets, with: *What did we do? Did we just ruin our lives?*

Then after it airs, almost immediately things go to another level.

They start doing TV, and even my mom and dad get involved. Since they live right near JFK, if the guys need lobster for a TV appearance in New York, they have it dropped off at my parents' house, and at seven thirty the next morning there's Sabin and Jim and the lobster on *The Today Show* or *Good Morning America*. My parents are solidly blue collar—dad works for Con Ed, my mom is a cafeteria worker in

New York's Catholic high schools—so for them this is almost otherworldly, but they love it.

Meanwhile, the conversations about my own possible involvement have been going on from the beginning. The question is what I would do. What would make sense for me to move out west and be part of this? So far the only notion that's come up was to maybe do a line of Cousins Maine Lobster apparel—T-shirts, hats, flip-flops, whatever—and I could oversee that.

But then, through Barbara, there comes the idea of franchising. And now they're asking me to come out and help launch that.

Frankly, I have real trepidation. I'm thirty-three years old, I grew up in Queens and lived my whole life in New York, and to be honest I'm not all that intrigued by California. So I'll be leaving my life behind to take on something I know absolutely nothing about. My dad, who's old school, is completely against it. He's like, *C'mon, you're gonna move across the country to work on a FOOD TRUCK?*

But Sabe can be pretty convincing. He's always Mr. Bright Side, and he's all *Trust me, trust me, trust me.*

And, frankly, my dad's doubts are all that much more motivation to do it and make sure it works.

I move to LA on August 31, 2014, by which time the LLC and the rest of the legal stuff is set up, and I'm raring to go. Sabin's sent me a bunch of calendar invites for trainings, so the first morning I show up at the office with my pad and pen and my best professional demeanor, ready to start learning the business.

Sabin looks at me and says, "What're you doing?"

"Well, you know, I'm here for the training."

He laughs. "Dude, I was shitting you, there is no training. I have no fucking clue how we're gonna do this. Now get out of my office and figure it out."

The next thing that happens, like the very next day, I meet Barbara, who tells me if I fuck up she'll chop off my balls.

But my attitude wasn't *What have I gotten myself into?* It was the opposite. I was relishing the challenge. If I was a deer in the headlights, there was nowhere else I'd rather be.

JIM

Learning a New Business, Again

Franchising is incredibly tough. We basically have to master a whole new business within the food truck industry. In addition to the legal complexities, there are the practical issues of maintaining brand integrity and learning to exercise what we'll come to call the franchise muscle—i.e., being an asshole when you have to be, but in a nice way.

These are all skills that, once learned, have to be continually fine-tuned and perfected.

Sabin's buddy Shaun Higgins has taken a major, major haircut to help out. I don't even know if he has a title, maybe franchise coordinator, maybe something else. But whatever it is, when he gets to LA, his office is what used to be a closet. There are filing cabinets and a fridge and freezer in there, leaving about eight inches for him to squeeze against the wall to reach the desk. It's actually easier for him to crawl under the desk to reach his chair. Fortunately, he's an athlete.

The first question is how to put the word out that Cousins Maine Lobster is franchising to potential franchisees. Generally this is a huge problem for a new franchisor unless they have millions of dollars to drop on advertising, and even then it's a roll of the dice.

But we have a solution, once again thanks to Barbara. Knowing that *Shark Tank* is always on the lookout for new angles, she suggests we request a follow-up appearance. She helps us craft the pitch, the producers approve it, and in the filmed piece we tell them not only that Cousins Maine Lobster has already expanded from one truck to four in Los Angeles, but that we're now going to have trucks all over the country through franchising.

We get thousands of leads and suddenly we are in the franchise business. Obviously, a lot of them are just tire kickers, but plenty are legit. Since it's just us three guys in the office, and we're not about to pay someone in-house fifty or sixty thousand dollars to field calls that may or may not turn into a franchise, we get a third-party broker out of Orange County to whittle down the prospects, working on commission. The way it works is, if he decides a prospect is legitimate and might be a good fit—if the prospect has liquidity and the necessary cash, and sincere interest in the brand—he'll vet the prospect over the phone and also look into what the market might be. And if everything checks out, there'll be a call with me.

This first call is something I started doing at this early stage and still do now, getting an initial gut reaction.

Then, if I pass the prospect, they'll be awarded with a Discovery Day, where they come to our office in Los Angeles and spend the day with me, Sabin, and Shaun. They go to one of our trucks for lunch, taste our food, and generally see the setup. We don't show anything that's proprietary, but enough to convey the idea, and for them to decide if they're excited to see themselves doing it—and for us to watch them the whole time.

We also do a tutorial where they see what the business will be like day in, day out. These days we have a dedicated six-person team in Maine to train franchisees and do a very thorough and exhaustive rundown about the business, the brand, the product, the sourcing, and how to make every single menu item; plus A to Z on the trucks, from the generator on down. But at the time, the sum total is a few minutes with our $14-hourly employees on the trucks, some of whom just work part-time.

Then we take a break in the afternoon, so they can relax and shower, after which we take them to dinner, followed by drinks at a bar. Back then, it's Barney's Beanery in West Hollywood, near where we live. And it's mainly because we believe in family first, and we want to see, if they get through this process, that we'll be comfortable kicking back with them outside of business and talking about family, kids, or vacation stuff. But it also has utility, because drinking tends to loosen people up, and oftentimes they'll reveal parts of themselves they've kept hidden.

It probably never occurs to big corporations to employ this tactic, but it's always worked for the three of us. Franchise applicants will say stupid shit, except to them it's the truth, what they really believe, or maybe their language will get really off-color. I remember one group who seem great all day, and we're like *Wow, these people will be fantastic.* Then we go out drinking and the guy starts telling us about all his DUIs, and I'm like, okay, maybe not someone we want to get in bed with.

Meanwhile, we know the waitresses at Barneys, and we ask them to join in a little experiment we do with prospects. We have food come out overcooked, or have them bring the wrong order completely, or just screw up their drinks to see how they'll react. Will they take it in stride and be kind, or is it gonna be *Fuck this, what the hell's wrong with you people?*

I mean, dealing with stuff going wrong without losing your shit is a huge part of the hospitality business, right?

Only if a prospect makes it through the whole process and that person winds up being awarded a franchise does our guy in Orange County get paid a commission on that sale.

Anyway, we finally get the ten: Phoenix, Raleigh, Houston, Dallas, Orlando, Atlanta, Napa Valley, San Diego, Nashville, and Las Vegas.

Going in, each group pays a $25,000 franchise fee (it's gone up twice since, and is now $40,000), and of course they've also got the cost of the food trucks, which go for between $90,000 and $110,000 used, and as much as twice that new.

Our new franchisees split used/new about evenly, though we don't hesitate to point out that buying new will probably ultimately end up saving money by keeping them on the road and steadily earning. Because even if everything in a used truck has been built perfectly—the insulation, the wiring, the technology—you're still driving an old chassis with a whole other set of problems. And we've learned the hard way that if your generator's busted, you're losing money not only in canceled events and product waste but in ruined relationships with bookers and coordinators.

So we give them the option to buy new. We've started looking for a truck builder as soon as the franchise requests started flooding in, because, holy shit, we're not about to use the guy we had to babysit.

What we're after is a professional outfit that'll do every truck the same way every time, rinse and repeat.

I start googling and researching and vetting. When I see there's one in Alabama that looks promising, I fly down there to look them over. They give me the full tour, and it's a pretty phenomenal operation. But I don't choose them, for the simple reason I can't stand the owner. He's an egotistical prick, and I have a pretty good idea that if we do business it's always gonna be his way or the highway, and who the hell needs that?

Meanwhile, we have an inquiry on our website from a truck building company—they've seen us on *Shark Tank*, and they figure we probably need help with these franchises we're building. And, by the way, they do the Salvation Army's trucks.

We get on the phone, and they sound terrific. And they say they're ready to drive to LA to talk further. I'm like, holy shit, driving seven hours from Phoenix to Los Angeles for a meeting, *that's* commitment! And then they do—in a Salvation Army truck, literally parking it right outside our office on Wilshire Boulevard! Sabin and I get in the truck; it's spic-and-span, beautifully wrapped. I mean, the Salvation Army, what more do you need to know?

So we go down to their facility, which checks out—big warehouse, lots of office space, people working on the floor, all this shit being built, all the bells and whistles.

Fine, we sign on the dotted line. From our perspective, it couldn't be better. For the first time all our trucks will be uniform, and they'll be in towns all over the country.

When we tell the franchisees, they're also stoked. They pay their money and eagerly wait for their trucks to roll off the line.

Some of the decisions we make in this transition to franchising will prove really smart—starting with the choice to begin with only the ten franchisees, which gives us the chance to test out the model even as we're learning the basics ourselves.

But this one is disastrous.

CHAPTER 12

Double Betrayal

CRYING ON THE INSIDE

SABIN

Let's put it this way: One moment everything seems to be going according to plan. We've got our ten franchisees, everyone's enthusiastic, and we can't wait to get started.

The first truck goes to Phoenix, Arizona, and they have a problem right out of the gate. Though it doesn't rain a lot in Phoenix, there's a downpour now—and we get a panicked call from our franchisee that rain is pouring through the roof of this brand-new truck.

We sit there watching the video with our mouths open. Like, *What the . . . ?*

But it's got to be an aberration, right?

The Phoenix franchisees are a mom-and-pop situation, and they don't know what the hell's going on. Neither do we. But what we do know is that, like the others, they've trusted us completely with their investment.

A few days later, the second truck gets delivered to Napa, and it's the same thing! Now the rainwater's rushing in over the hood, and pissing on the grill.

I reassure everyone—including the other franchisees, who are hearing about this as they wait for their own trucks—that we'll straighten it out. But already I'm starting to realize that's not going to be so easy. I'm already getting into yelling matches with the truck building guy, who's talking a load of crap: *Don't worry, no big deal, we'll fix it.*

Incredibly, it's only now that we do what we should have done months earlier: a fucking three-minute Google search. Because what it reveals is a slew of complaints against the company from others who've been ripped off and oh yes . . . lawsuits.

It is a nightmare, and it keeps getting worse.

When they stop returning our calls, we file a lawsuit, and they initially answer. Only later will we realize it was only to stall things and force us to waste money.

Still, even now we're clinging to the faint hope they'll somehow try to make it right. Partly it's because we're still getting random emails assuring us they're on pace for the next truck.

But it's also because the alternative is still so hard to believe: that all of it—the Salvation Army trucks, their impressive facility—was total bullshit all along.

Then, again, it's likely they were so convincing because they believed it.

The truth is, even after all this time we don't have the full story on the truck building company. Clearly at one point they did build some trucks that were legitimate, even if on closer inspection they were probably dog-shit quality.

Either way, we are the perfect pigeons. It's hard to overstate how naïve we are when launching the franchising business, and how totally unprepared to protect ourselves. We don't have a legal team—hell, we don't even have an attorney. Obviously we didn't even do minimal background or credit checks. Young and aggressive as we are, what we're mainly interested in is getting things done fast, and with the least possible bother. There's basically just the three of us, and we have a million other things going on at the same time, including running our LA trucks on a day-to-day basis.

At the risk of repeating myself, we're fucking idiots.

And, then, the final blow. One day we find out, *poof,* they're gone. They've just closed down and left—for, as we soon discover, Honduras. With everyone's money. More than a million dollars!

Why Honduras? Well, it turns out they own a bar down there, as well as some other property. And a million-plus dollars goes pretty far in Honduras.

To say we're mortified doesn't begin to tell it. The shame is almost unbearable. After all, these franchisees have trusted us. They've put their lives in our hands, plus in some cases their life savings.

We hide nothing. We tell them everything right away, and it's as bad as you can imagine. Up to now they've been looking at us as these very smart, charismatic young men, and now, suddenly, we're total fuckups who don't know shit about business, and their money is gone!

Every day I think the same thing: Imagine if this happened to someone in my family. Imagine if they saw something on TV, and *because* it's on TV, it has to be rock-solid. So you see our pitch, and you say *Oh my God, I love this idea,* and you tell your wife, and she supports it, you go and take a risk on this business with these two cousins from Maine who seem so appealing on TV, because you believe in it and in them.

You pay $120,000 and you hire staff, do all the training, and announce to your community that you'll be open January 5. Then the truck doesn't come, and you learn the guy has shut his business down and gone to Honduras—you've lost your life savings and the idiots you put your faith in didn't do a simple background check.

Because that's pretty much what happened.

I'll never forget getting a call from the franchisee in Raleigh, Greg. It comes just as Shaun and I are pulling our food truck into Coachella, as we're vending at the concert. Greg isn't rude, just direct. "How are you gonna get back my life savings?" he wants to know. "Listen," I tell him, "I know you don't know me well, and you've got plenty of reasons not to trust me. But I *guarantee* you, I will make this right. Either you will get your money back or you will get a truck. I will NOT let you down."

Because as far as I'm concerned, this disaster is totally on me. I should have done a lot more research on these assholes, and then afterward kept a lot closer tabs on them, and I didn't.

So for me it couldn't be more personal. No one else can unfuck this, not even Barbara. It's MY responsibility; I'VE gotta do whatever it takes to fix it. These people put their lives in our hands, and if we don't do right by them, it's the end of the company.

Jimmy gets it. He knows me well enough to know that for my own sanity I have to control every element of this fight, and he lets me do it.

In fact, if anything, this whole miserable situation will only strengthen our bond. There's no finger-pointing, and no one ever loses his temper, none of that. Our attitude is: We're at war and we've got to win.

And over the next year and a half, that's how it goes.

First, we have to do right—or as right as we can—by the franchisees. Greg, in Raleigh, gets one of the trucks we've been using in LA. For the others, we beg and borrow and go on starvation wages to get them back their money so that, with our blessing, they can have their trucks built locally and belatedly launch their businesses. At least for now, our hope for uniform trucks has to go down the drain.

We give the local truck builders our specs and layouts, and they more or less follow the blueprint—here's where the windows are, here's where the equipment goes. It's far from perfect, but it's a temporary fix.

Meanwhile I'm going after the bastards down in Honduras full tilt. I hire the best law firm in Phoenix. Lawsuits get filed; subpoenas get issued. I hire a private investigator to try and track down what properties they own, and if they can be attached to the lawsuit.

Every day I'm on the phone with lawyers six or seven or ten hours, getting to know the legal system backward and forward, learning by doing, and it turns out I'm really good at it. But it's exhausting. And I literally hurt physically. The minute my eyes open in the morning my heart is going through my chest, and after being on the phone with lawyers all day, I go straight to the bar and drink and eat until the moment at night my eyes close. Because the only way I can go to sleep is by drinking. Over the next year I gain, like, twenty pounds.

How we don't lose our business I'll never know, it's just a miracle.

At first the truck builder guys ignore us. They know how hard it is for the victims in cases like this to get anything resembling justice even if they're in America.

With white-collar crime, unless it's huge, absolutely no one cares. Not the FBI, that's for sure; when I contact them, they won't give me the time of day. Still, though the feds barely respond, we make sure word reaches Honduras that they're involved, if only to spook them.

But the deeper I go into these guys, the clearer it is they've *never* played by the rules.

In fact, in the end, one of my big takeaways from the whole thing is to stop being so careful about the rules myself. Like I used to get worried if I got a notice in the mail from, say, the city of Santa Monica, saying I have to reply by July 9, and follow such and such a procedure or face such and such consequences, and I'd be like, *Oh my God, I gotta reply immediately!* Now it's like, no, *I'll reply when I want to reply.*

So these people taught me a lot actually; they gave me an invaluable legal education. It is so hard to actually shut someone down for wrongdoing, it taught me that we, as good guys, could occasionally make a mistake and not be punished with the death penalty.

For a long time the whole thing is demoralizing, and there are definitely times when I think the bad guys are gonna win.

But I'm relentless and can't let myself think that way. Okay, no way we'll put them behind bars, but we've got to get the money back.

Though one thing we've learned by now is that they definitely have resources, property in the States as well as in Honduras. But they're not stupid, they've covered their tracks, and nothing is in their name. We find one house they put in Grandma's name, and they retitled it multiple times.

But their mistake—and our break—is that to get tax breaks and do some other shit, they put their kids on all their business LLCs. But all's fair, you do what you gotta do. So when we sued and won, we got to garnish the kids' wages to collect the judgment and start taking their money out of every paycheck.

That's when the father decides to answer the phone and settle.

It took years, but we didn't get fatigued and give up like they expected, and in the end, I got the money back. All of it.

I know now I could have spent half the price on the legal process, but that, too, I chalk up to experience. Because the lessons learned were worth all of that and more—hard lessons about human nature and about business. It made us a lot smarter and stronger.

At least for me, the whole ordeal took a psychological toll that endures to this day. It's always there, an undercurrent of negativity and inability to trust people. A few people had warned us from the beginning that you can't run a business with a culture based on trust and friendship; they were right, and we were wrong. There wasn't a more important lesson to learn, or probably a worse way to learn it.

But, my God, even now it makes me really sad.

If I think about the negative experiences we've had over the years as bricks in a wall—the times a trusted employee stole us blind, the time another started a competing lobster business—this would be at least fifty bricks. It was fucking horrible. *Horrible.*

And it would have ripple effects.

JIM

The Coup

For me, the worst day of the truck builder horror show was the one just before Thanksgiving 2014. Our extended family is out west for the holiday—my mom and dad; Sabin's mom, Jeannie; a bunch of cousins; and they're all sitting in Sabe's grandmother's living room, none of them knowing anything yet about what's going on.

Meanwhile, in the next room the two of us are on the phone with this creep. We're trying to keep ourselves under control, but we're just at the breaking point; *we're in bed with horrible people, it's clear. They're never going to fix the crappy trucks they've delivered, let alone build any more.*

So we can't help ourselves. We just start unloading on these guys, demanding our money back. And of course their attitude—*Fuck you, good luck with that!*—gets us even angrier.

By the time we hang up, I'm completely spent and as depressed as I've ever been in my life. Everything's gone to shit, and there are all kinds of ways it could go from here, all of them bad. But now we plaster smiles on our faces and it's: *OK, let's go do family dinner.*

Of course they've heard the whole thing, so now we have to deal with *that*—in my case, specifically my mom. She's worried not just about my livelihood but for my safety, because who the hell knows what these people are capable of?

Fortunately my dad is his usual levelheaded self. His message: *Yes, it's bad, but you just have to work through it. And, fine, if you don't want to do that, if it's too hard, then don't. But don't complain.*

It's not that different from what we're hearing from Barb, who tells us that her best entrepreneurs are the ones that don't waste time feeling bad for themselves. They just get up as quickly as possible and figure it the fuck out.

But she also adds something else: that of all those she's backed, we're gonna be the quickest to make it big.

Between the two of them, it's the best guidance we could have gotten. Because what's coming will be brutal beyond belief.

I'd be in the office every night 'til eleven or midnight—between the legal stuff, and dealing with the pissed-off franchisees on top of our usual workload—and I'd just stare up at the ceiling, thinking, *Holy shit, how great would it be to be in Boston right now?!*

Basically, Sabin, Shaun, and I are the Three Musketeers—united but miserable. We'll have a break maybe once every couple of weeks when we go to a bar and blow off steam, but otherwise it's just working, working, working, trying to make it through that tunnel and looking for the light.

But there are times I'm not sure I'll make it. One time I'm talking to my mom and dad en route to an event in Brentwood, and suddenly I just break down, sobbing. And I tell them, *Listen, I'm probably gonna be home soon, and you'll also probably be seeing us on* Dateline *for the wrong reasons.*

Which of course freaks my mom out. And then, when I get to the venue, I have to walk out of the car and pretend to the people eating our lobster and the staff in the truck that things couldn't be better.

That thing about being on *Dateline* was a grim joke among the three of us—the imaginary headline read *From Shark Tank to Dateline*—but we really were worried this mess could lead to serious legal trouble. So maybe *American Greed: Scams, Schemes, and Broken Dreams* would've been the better fit.

Either way, at that moment the worst of it wasn't the crooks in Honduras who were out to screw us, but our franchisees who are still pissed over all the shit they've had to endure. They're pissed and they're stressed, and for a time, with some of them, every conversation has threatening undertones.

I honestly don't blame them for feeling that way. Still, it's not like we haven't done everything in our power to make them whole. Sabe's pounding away on the legal side, and I'm doing everything that I can to help them recoup and launch their businesses, however belatedly. We've helped them find alternative trucks—and while they're not by a long shot the ones we hoped for, at least they're on the road and generating income. For the Raleigh franchisee, we've even gone so far as to put one of our LA trucks on a flatbed truck and ship it across the country.

Basically, our stance has never changed: We're in this together. And now that you're up and running, let us help you succeed with the actual selling, because this is the part of the business we know really well.

But what we're finding is that with some of these ten first franchisees, there's no way to even begin to regain the lost trust.

There is a clear leader of the group, and he begins to form an alliance against us, and it feels horrible. Horrible is an understatement, it is crushing. They orchestrate a group call, it must have lasted three hours, and it was cringeworthy.

When we get on the line with them we're totally blindsided. It's a mugging. Basically they want to completely redo the terms of the relationship. It's like, *We don't have to listen to you anymore, you've shown us that you're fucking idiots. Look how you screwed up!*

It's an outright coup, and it comes at the worst possible time—just when we're finally past the truck builder crisis and starting to hit our stride.

They have a long list of complaints and demands, starting with wanting us to reduce our royalty. But what they want even more is a reduction in what they're paying for the lobster meat.

They're not exactly subtle. They figure they can use our inexperience—and our genuine regret—to bully and browbeat us into bending.

And stunned as we are, we nearly do. Because we liked and trusted most of these people, and now there's just this absolute, overwhelming sense of betrayal.

The leader of the group, of course, is the loudest. He claims he's showing crazy losses on his P&Ls, $50,000 a month. And we're looking at his numbers and thinking there's no way he can be losing that much money; it's gotta either be for tax purposes or he's lying as ammunition to get us to revise the terms of his contract and bring down the price of his lobster.

Whatever it is, as it goes on it becomes obvious how abysmally ignorant he is of even the basics of the business. He doesn't even know how many ounces of meat go in his lobster roll.

But he's gotten the other franchises involved, and even though they were doing pretty decent sales, he's convinced them they're all getting ripped off.

As the session goes on, it becomes clear the rest of them barely have a better grasp of the economics of the business than he does. For instance, the one franchisee tells us he's called US Foods, and their price is two dollars less per pound than we're selling at. It's like he doesn't even get that there's as wide a variety of quality as with any other type of protein. I mean, you can get a filet at a top steakhouse, or you can get a filet at Chili's; and they're both filets, but they're different cuts, different grades, different treatments through the processing plant, different everything, starting with the actual animal.

It's actually surprising how much our angry franchisees don't know, or at least fail to appreciate, about the business we're in together. The fact is, what they're paying for is quality, sourcing, and the brand. Because while a lot of others use lobsters that go into holding tanks cracked or damaged, we only use those just off the boat, claws snapping and tails flapping, the liveliest, healthiest, and sweetest tasting.

Nor do they understand the innumerable reasons market prices can shift so wildly:

- The variables of weather. For while at any given moment there might be lots of lobsters on the ocean floor, if it's crazy windy, or storming, the guys can't go out as far, or haul in as many traps, but *their* costs for everything from the bait used in the traps to fuel prices are constant.
- The unpredictability of competition for product. For instance, China is a big buyer of live lobster, so we often have to contend with China's open checkbook; but when tariffs on American seafood were imposed on China, for a while they were out of the game, so domestic prices fell dramatically. Then there are the cruise lines, which, when they are doing well, are great for us. Why? Because they're huge buyers of lobster *tails*, and when lobster tails are moving, the meat we're after—the claws and knuckles—is more available. But the opposite is also true. When the cruise lines were hurting during COVID, our costs went through the roof.

These are among the many things that haven't been even a blip on most of the franchisees' radar. Their only focus is price—which has made it all too easy for this guy leading the coup to poison the well.

Then, again, it's *our* problem that we failed to convey all this information to them a lot earlier.

There will be a number of lessons we'll learn from this miserable experience, but maybe the most important of them is the need to educate our franchisees. Starting in 2015, what before had been a perfunctory introduction to the company and the product becomes a full-on training program.

Franchisees go to Maine and they see the whole process, from the lobsters being harvested on the ocean floor to the moment the roll goes out the truck window, and absolutely everything in between. They speak to lobstermen and our processors and see how hard the work is, and learn why prices move, and the nuances of the supply chain.

They come to see themselves as partners in our company, and they understand that we're doing something different here. That this is indeed about quality and the customer experience, and what we're focusing on is its being the same in every city, so that the super high expectations created by what you ate three years ago in Pittsburgh will be met in Florida today.

And that's more meaningful to them than trying to save a couple of bucks and having some shit meat that no one will come back for.

CHAPTER 13

Two Steps Forward, One Step Back

FAMILY

SABIN

Between the truck issue and the coup, those first couple of years franchising were so rough. But on the plus side, they taught us a lot about ourselves. And what we learned is that no matter what gets thrown at us, we're not gonna break.

In one sense, we'd been lucky. Devastating as those events were to live through, they'd drawn little outside notice in the media or anywhere else. Which is to say, now that we've regained our equilibrium and are moving forward, the public fallout is close to nonexistent.

The task immediately at hand was figuring out who among the original franchisees was going to stay part of the organization. That was huge. We'd started with the idea that these ten would serve as our proof of concept, bringing each of them on with high hopes and expectations. We weren't interested in just taking their money; the point was to make sure they were successful, so they'd be part of a solid organization based on trust and mutual support.

Yeah, okay, they had their reasons. We badly screwed up. No question, it was traumatic for them also. But rather than bringing us closer together, they'd listened to this little birdie bitching in their ear and leading the coup against us. Suddenly our business was no good, and supposedly they couldn't make money unless we renegotiated the terms they'd signed on to.

It's hard enough to build a franchise brand when everything's lovey-dovey, but it's almost impossible if franchisees don't operate under an agreed-upon set of rules and regulations. And how do you implement rules and regulations if the franchisees don't respect you?

It did help that afterward a couple of them called to apologize. But the others? They chose their side, and after that we'd never trust them again.

Yet as much as anything else, this was on us. It was another way we'd drastically fucked up. We thought we had the right people, and we were wrong about most of them. (I have no doubt they feel the same about us.) We thought we could have this culture of trust and friendship that would get us through the rough patches.

In fact, we now realize that what we have to be, in good times and bad, is tough businessmen. And not hesitate to weed out the bottom dwellers. If there's a bad egg—bad employee, bad manager, bad franchisee, bad anything—cut the cord.

And starting now, we had to be a whole lot smarter about who we partnered with.

We wanted the three who were loyal, Raleigh, Nashville, and Vegas, to stay with us. They did. Two are still franchisees today; both have done extremely well and we're very close to them.

The rest are gone. All the locales are still in operation, just under different owners.

Making that happen took time, about a year and a half, but it wasn't as painful as it might have been. The fact is, we liked most of these people. That's why we'd wanted them in the first place, and in most cases the feeling was mutual, so no one wanted outright conflict. At least *half chose to leave the franchising business on their own.* The guy in Dallas was an attorney who decided being a lawyer is what he actually liked being, rather than an entrepreneur; he gladly transferred his business to our new Houston guy. Meanwhile the Orlando guy decided he was more a brick-and-mortar type than a roaming food truck guy, and he also sold to a new group. Then there was Carrie out of Phoenix, a nice lady who reminded us of our mothers—but, hey, our mothers wouldn't want to run a food truck, either; so she was taken over by our Nashville franchisee. The Napa guy left too.

I'm not saying learning these lessons doesn't harden you. It does, it numbs you out. I look at my mom, who's never run a business; she's just been an employee. She sees the good in every single person. Talk to a seasoned businessperson, and they damn well do *not* see good in every person. If they're good at what they do, they're more likely to suss out the bad. It's the difference between a person who dated one hundred people before they got married and the person who married their high school sweetheart: Which one is more likely to be surprised that someone's cheating or that the relationship otherwise goes to shit?

These days I have no trouble at all firing someone. Just a couple of months ago I had to fire a senior executive, and I happened to tell my son, who's eight. He asked, *What does that mean?* I told him, and he couldn't believe it. He was really upset. *You shouldn't have done that*, he said, *that's mean*. That's a kid's perspective, and it should be. But the truth is, if I made any mistake in that situation, it is that I waited so long. I should have fired her eight months ago.

Does that sound harsh? I guess. But one thing the whole experience with the trucks and the first group of franchisees drove home, if I needed any reminding, is how special this thing we've created is. It's not like we've opened the latest hamburger hut and are just trying to make as much money as fast as we can, or mass producing oatmeal raisin cookies. If we screwed up then and had to close the business, no one gives a shit.

But we know what we have. We're sitting here holding a very rare diamond in our hand—and we almost fumbled it.

Aside from everything else, we know how many people are behind us. We're from a very small state that maybe doesn't have too much to brag about, and because we were visible on TV and became overnight sensations, everyone was supportive, cheering us on. I mean, this business has a passion, and an ethos, that's *meaningful*. There is something truly special at Cousins Maine Lobster, and everyone that's here is a part of this giant, wild journey.

We're constantly aware of how close we came to losing all that, and ever since, that awareness has figured in every decision we make.

Today those crises feel like ancient history. When new people come into our business now, the respect is pretty much built in. They see we know what we're doing, and that we're good at it—it's ding ding ding, check, check, check, right down the line. They also know that if they fuck with us, we have lawyers up the wazoo. We'll know what to do, and it probably won't be good for them.

JIM

Find Your People

The question now becomes what to look for in the next batch of franchisees—and who to avoid.

There are still plenty of candidates eager to sign up, few of whom know or care about our screwups. But of course this time we're looking at these potential partners with different eyes.

For all the pain involved with the coup, it undeniably clarified a couple of things—starting with how stupid we'd been in our methodology for selecting franchisees. Yes, it was now obvious that most were far from natural entrepreneurs, and some had gotten involved impetuously, with only the vaguest sense of the business or what it would take to make a serious go of it. But what was our basis for bringing them in? Mainly that they seemed like nice people who'd fit into our Cousins Maine Lobster "family." And little matters like, oh, for instance, *the strength of their financials* were an almost secondary consideration.

So the task now, as we go about slotting in replacement owners and selectively adding new ones, is finding people who have both the means and mindset to run their businesses the right way. Individuals or groups well enough capitalized to ride out the slow times, and smart enough to manage their teams.

As usual for us, we have to figure this out the hard way.

If there's an initial model for the kind of owner we're after, it has to be our new guy in Houston, the one who's taken over the Dallas franchise. He looks like a total winner. His new business in Houston is prospering—starting with two trucks, he's already looking to expand to five.

Except it soon turns out he's financed that expansion by bringing in big-money lenders as partners; and then, finding himself in a hole, he's screwed the partners and filed for bankruptcy. The whole thing fell apart—we go from five trucks in Houston back down to one, and we end up transferring that operation to a *new* franchisee. (Happily he's done well and is still there, and ten years later, they've grown it back up to three.)

Still, at that moment, all at once we're down to ten trucks total, in all locales, when we thought we'd have fourteen. And while in the interim we've sold franchises in five other territories, it will be six or eight months before those trucks get built and on the road and start generating royalties.

And it's becoming clear this is how it's going to go for a while. Not steady upward growth, but the classic two steps forward, one step back. On the one hand, everywhere we go people are crazy about the product; in every new territory—Pittsburgh, Cleveland, or wherever—the reaction's the same. Yet with every encouraging development there tends to be a negative one sneakily sitting around the corner. We are in the battle of getting through the muck and gaining true steam, and that process is trying, but worth it in the end.

So, yes, we're growing, but it's not gonna be steady like we hoped, from ten trucks to fifteen to twenty to twenty-five; it's gonna be from ten to fifteen, to seventeen, back to thirteen, then twenty, and back again to seventeen.

Basically it becomes a matter of weeding out the problems—either the wrong people or wrong market, or the right person who's gotten overextended thinking he could handle more than one truck, and all kinds of other variations.

Every time we're hit with a new one, and probably lose another truck, it can't help but create a bit of concern about the long-term viability of the company. I mean, I remember going back and forth about whether to get a new apartment that cost $400 more a month—and I decided I'd better not.

Under the best of circumstances, assessing someone's potential to succeed as a franchisee would be an inexact science. Between the non-stop workload and all the built-in uncertainties, it's just something very few people are cut out for.

So there's always a high degree of guesswork. Over the years, there have been some franchisees I considered barely okay who turned out to be amazing, and plenty of others who were the opposite.

That said, we're a helluva lot better at picking winners today than we were back then. We're much more thorough in our background and credentials checks, and we're better at asking the right questions to solicit the right kind of information.

Yes, we still take them out drinking to see if they'll spill the beans. But what we mainly do better these days is listen. After all this time, we can talk to a prospect on the phone and, with our large body of experience, immediately draw comps to someone else from five or eight or thirteen years ago. So after one of those conversations, one of us might say, *Man, he sounds like a lot of fun, but doesn't he remind you of that guy who we thought was gonna be great and ended up being so annoying?* Or it might be, *My God, they're totally dialed in, they've got a great work ethic, they really get the marketing and the booking the truck part.*

In general, we've just gotten really good at following our guts and being able to distinguish the genuine from the BS. We're in accord probably 90% of the time, immediately aligned on who's gonna be a good fit. And that other 10% is just as valuable, because it makes us stop and think about it some more and reassess.

All that said, the most fundamental question of all never changes: Is this someone I'd want to work for? And if the answer is no, then we're not gonna do it, both because we know that person will be a cancer in the organization, and we know they're not going to be successful anyway. Why? Because if you're an asshole, no one's gonna want to work for you.

This is not mere speculation—we *have* had franchisees give up because they couldn't staff their trucks.

The process is organic. As time has gone by and the brand has continued to build, we've attracted a better and better caliber of franchisee: people who are better capitalized, with more entrepreneurial and business savvy, who can run trucks remotely and understand how to chase bookings and sales because they've built a strong team. People who know that if you do it right, the money will come.

And they're fun to work for, so their people don't get burned out.

There are all kinds of elements we look for to make sure our company is strong and solid, but that's always foremost.

At the same time we've learned to be on the lookout for red flags—the people who want in just for the hell of it or to chase what they think is an easy buck. For instance, we recently had a prospect who, on paper, couldn't look better. He has more money than I'll ever see—owns thirty Wendy's and twenty Dunkin' Donuts. And when we first started talking, he was an obvious "yes."

But over the course of a few weeks, we started seeing his arrogant side—he couldn't help telling us what we needed to do for him and how we needed to do it. Well, I don't care how much money you have, or how much money we can make off you, because over the long term you'll be a detriment to the other franchisees who are part of this business and wear their hearts on their sleeve for this brand.

At the other extreme, there's another new prospect from California we're getting to know. He's a guy who works his Subway businesses side by side with his wife and, man, does that ever resonate with me! And we've also got these new guys from Wisconsin who've also made a great first impression. When they come to see us, they don't want a fancy dinner, they're happier with a freaking burger at a bar. But mainly they're just raring to get in the trenches.

That's the kind of people we can count on being part of our business's foundation.

SHAUN HIGGINS

It was 2015 that we began focusing most of our efforts on building and supporting a network of franchisees. That's when we sold two of our four LA trucks and, while ten years later we still have the remaining two as well as six others nationally, since then franchising has been our main business.

Still, it wasn't until 2018 that the company truly began to become what it is today. First, we had to work through the truck issue, and after that the fallout from the coup, so it took us a couple of years to solidify the original ten and prove the model. But throughout that time we were also mastering the nuances of franchising and enhancing the team. By 2018 it had all come together. We had a really solid group of franchisees and had the corporate structure to begin pushing a little harder on the gas pedal.

At that point we brought in a bunch of really exceptional franchisees, in locales across the country. They've all done extremely well and have been major brand ambassadors for the company.

Of course there was an element of luck, but not really a very large one. As a result of our early experience we've been very, very careful in granting franchises. We respond to every application in a timely fashion and would hate to overlook someone special—I mean, is that guy who applies at two in the morning for real or just hammered? But overall we're just very intentional and very methodical, because we have an identity as a company that we cherish. It reflects who we are, and we're not only about chasing numbers.

We end up granting franchises to no more than 10% of prospects, if that. We've had groups ready to throw major money at the business and scale it; and if that's what we were after, we could easily have thousands of units. But we don't, because success in this business not only takes a ton of care and commitment, it takes embracing a philosophy and even a lifestyle.

Once you become part of Cousins Maine Lobster you become part of the Maine lobster industry. You'll absorb every detail of how the product gets from the trap to our trucks. You'll go out on the boats with the lobstermen, and some days it'll be calm, crystal-clear water, and some days you'll be sick to your stomach before you're five hundred yards out, but, here's the thing, you won't want to pass even on those days.

What do we look for in potential franchisees?

Let's put it this way: Mainly things we can't teach. I can teach somebody how to operate a food truck and how to physically handle our lobster meat. I can educate them about the industry and about Maine and how to put together financial statements. What I can't teach them is how to work really hard or how to be genuinely warm. Those are the people we want, not just because they'll succeed—which they will—but because we're gonna be spending a lot of time with them.

I'm talking about people like Yunus Shahul. He arrived in this country maybe twenty years ago from India, hoping to get into the film industry, and when that didn't work out, he really struggled. He was actually sleeping in the New York subway for a while, between odd jobs at gas stations and restaurants. But after he was finally hired full-time by an Indian restaurant, he learned the owner was looking for additional revenue streams, and that got him going.

Yunus suggests they get a truck to sell the restaurant's food. He's put in charge of it, builds out the truck, does all the permits and licensing, and puts it on the road, and it does fine. But one day he has the truck at an event, and he spots a Cousins Maine Lobster truck with a long line out front. He's so intrigued, he leaves his truck to others and hangs out all day watching our operation. And before the day's over, he's submitted a franchise request to us online.

A few weeks later, he comes out to LA, and immediately I'm struck by how he's at once humble and super passionate. Having seen our trucks only from the outside, he's completely blown away when he actually gets to board one; but not as much as we are, when we see he already knows his way around all our specialized equipment.

Cut to seven years later. Among the many successful owners in our system, Yunus is probably the most successful of all. He's got a massive operation, currently runs twenty-four trucks out of seven districts of operation—New York; Connecticut; Maryland; Virginia; Chicago; Florida; Washington, DC—with a ton of employees to oversee social media, bookings, scheduling, all that stuff. The last time I checked in with him, he had 120-plus employees. He's so good—and has such faith in his people—that he actually launched trucks in Chicago and Florida on the same weekend.

How much does a guy like that bring in a year? Well, figure that our goal is for franchisees to profit somewhere between 10% and 15%, each truck on average generating around $1.3 million. So do the math. He does very well.

But here's the thing: He never stops seeing himself as part of the larger CML family. He's always ready to get on the phone to reassure new prospects overwhelmed by what they're getting into, or to share his experiences with older ones about what's worked and what to stay away from.

Of course, we're extremely hands-on with the franchisees ourselves. This is a two-way street, and they know we are *always* available. Straightforward as it looks from the outside, when a new owner comes aboard there's an enormous amount to learn, and we need to teach it to them without overwhelming them.

That of course begins with the orientation program, It is sixteen weeks, divided between Maine, where we have seven trainers offering instruction in all things lobster related; and Nashville, where we have in place operational models of the truck kitchens, enabling franchisees to get comfortable with the equipment and the range of menu items, as well as learn in that controlled environment how to handle volume, and the stress that can come with glancing out the window at long lines of customers.

Following the first disastrous experience, obviously we were very careful, but we hit the jackpot with our current truck guy. Not only are the trucks themselves extremely well built and, when ordered, come with every bell and whistle, but the guy hits every completion date; then after delivery continues to remain available. If there's an issue with the truck, or if the franchisee simply has a question, he always picks up the phone. He's even been able to help certain groups with financing, leading to their getting approved, like, *immediately.*

In short, he, too, has become an invaluable partner.

Once a franchisee is in operation, our team checks in with them on a weekly basis, though they of course know they don't need to wait a week to call us about anything at all.

We also encourage them to bring us their ideas. Sabe, Jim, and myself, our entire team, none of us has an ego or claims to know everything and, in fact, some of our best ideas have come from franchisees. It might be something as simple as suggesting, as one did, that we share KPI reports, so everyone knows where he stacks up versus others in the system, and what changes—say, in operating hours—might enhance results. So we first started producing those reports monthly, then made it weekly.

The San Francisco franchisees came to us with the idea of putting an 85-inch TV on the side of their truck. It was around the time of the NBA playoffs and these guys, they're a pair of brothers, wanted to stream Warriors games for waiting customers, figuring they might also use the TV in other ways, like displaying menus.

Brilliant idea! We tested it out with them, and now we require TVs on all our trucks. While they can't be used to show sports without approval, the idea grew into having a tech stack that streams videos of Maine and tells the story of the company; or if we're launching a new whoopie pie flavor or garlic butter lobster roll, it can be used to promote that.

In addition to the trucks, there are also two brick-and-mortar locations in the system, one in Asbury Park, New Jersey, the other on the San Francisco pier. Both joined the business as food truck owners, and they still have their trucks, but after falling in love with the business, they also wanted to do brick and mortar.

Asbury Park came first, launching in May 2022, and they really helped prove the concept after previous . . . *mistakes*. It really came down to location—in both cases, they wanted the right mix of tourists and locals, and before we locked into any leases, we brought in real estate professionals to make sure from their standpoint these were the right spots.

Another real growth area has been the e-commerce division. It's always been an option—since the original *Shark Tank* pitch meeting, where it ended up on the cutting room floor—but it's become much more of a focus in the last few years, after we launched Cousins Seafood Distribution and could have inventory space and our fridges and freezers under our own roof.

Hard to believe that when I arrived in LA in August 2012 to help launch the franchising operation, I was Cousins Maine Lobster's first employee, with no title and a closet for an office.

But even harder to believe is that I considered not taking the leap for even a moment. I love being in LA; I met my fiancée in Newport Beach, it's a real community, and it reminds me of the way I grew up in Queens.

Both my parents are gone now, and I miss them terribly. But it's a blessing that they lived to see what CML turned into—and the part that I've played. And really, that would have been enough. But, then, in 2023, one night in Boston at our annual retreat for franchisees, all of us are at dinner in this terrific Italian restaurant, and suddenly Sabin and Jim stand up, and they announce they've named me company president. I had no clue, it just completely caught me off guard, and I was totally bowled over.

Obviously, I couldn't take the obligation more seriously. From the very first, through all the ups and down, I've regarded CML as my baby, to be protected and nurtured.

But it's also so *satisfying.*

Even after all this time, it's hard to express what it's like to watch one of our trucks hit a neighborhood or a town for the first time, and see all these grown men and women thrilled just to be standing in line and waiting, anticipating what's coming. It's like the way I used to feel at Six Flags Great Adventure, waiting two hours for the scream machine, and it's done in twenty seconds, but it's so special you don't care, you just want to do it again.

Well that's the business we're in, it's what we're giving them—ice cream for adults.

CHAPTER 14

Beyond the Business

SABIN

I got into the Big Brothers program back in Maine when I was thirteen. It couldn't have come at a better time, because I really needed it. Like I always say—and I say it now in speeches—I was one of those kids that could have gone either way; I flirted with good and bad, and I'm thankful to have finally found a good path.

My Big Brother's name was Steve Lacovara. We got matched after I'd been on the waitlist for two years, and if it had gone on any longer, who knows where I would be today?

Sheer blind luck. He was an Italian kid from Jersey, and he was in the Coast Guard at the time, stationed in Maine, and he happened to read about being a Big Brother in the *PennySaver* while doing laundry. So he signed up and got me.

It's not like we'd do anything earth-shattering—usually go get some food, hang out, and just talk. What guys do. But he was present, and I'd never had that before. He came to all of my games, and it was hugely impactful.

He was only twenty-two himself, only eight years older than me. Today, thirty years later, he's a highly decorated colonel in the Marines, and we're still very close. I was the best man at his wedding, and he named his son after me—Anthony Sabin Lacovara.

So every chance I get, I tell people to mentor children. I'm a two-time Big Brother myself—signed up the first time when I was twenty-seven or twenty-eight, and got a little brother named Lawrence, who's now an adult. So I started again, and now I've got a little brother named Khari. This is how important it is to me: I was doing it the whole time we were building the company, through all the ups and all the downs, even in the middle of crises.

In 2016, I was nominated by the Los Angeles branch and then voted national Big Brother of the Year. Lawrence and I actually got an invite to the White House, though unfortunately we ended up not going because it was the period of Obama transitioning to Trump and things got too chaotic.

Obviously, the whole concept of family is central to everything I do. Back in 2012, when we accepted Barbara's offer on *Shark Tank*, and blurted out to Barbara "Welcome to the family," it may have sounded like just a line, but it wasn't. To me that's what the company was always meant to be. That was the goal, to create a family. And to the extent we've been successful, it's because the people who are with us today, both our employees and our franchisees, share that vision; just as earlier the whole thing might've come crashing down largely because we got ourselves mixed up with people who didn't.

I mean, it's almost impossible to describe how great it is to be doing this not just with Jimmy but with my other two closest friends in the world, Shaun Higgins and Jake Mutscheller, who runs all of our corporate units. I've known Shaun since college, and I've known Jake even longer, since I was a kid. It's all come together to make an amazing culture. These two guys have the best hearts, they hold me accountable, and they have always been there for me. I owe them so much and I am so thankful to finally have the brothers I have always wanted.

The instability in my past was a particular problem with women. I always had girlfriends, always. But my upbringing caused me to be attracted to people who were not good matches. No surprise, I found unhealthy patterns.

Around the time we started franchising I was in a really toxic relationship. When work should have been the priority, dealing with this relationship was.

It was actually Shaun's mom who got me out of it. She called one day and flat-out said, "Sabin, I'm sorry to overstep my boundaries, but you need to break up with that girl. She's bad, she's very, *very* bad."

So I did, and I escaped by the skin of my teeth. And at that point I realized I had to really start thinking about what I was doing. People knew I was a budding businessman, they knew about the company, what am I doing with these random girls? I should be with someone the *opposite* of that, someone special.

What's strange, and it shows how messed up I was, is that I already knew that person: Erika, my now wife. She represents everything that I never knew growing up—normalcy, stability, kindness. She comes from a loving, two-parent family, and she's just an amazing person.

We met back when I didn't have a dollar to my name, working together in real estate. As a couple, we were on and off, because I wasn't ready to settle down, so I didn't give the relationship my all. But even so, she's a rock, always there for me when I need her. When I tore my Achilles tendon and was on crutches, she took me grocery shopping and carried it up to my second-story apartment. I mean, that's just who she is—kind and decent and thoughtful.

Erika is the true definition of a partner, a wife, a friend, and a trooper, always supporting me and allowing me to reach for new, higher goals. She is selfless and beautiful, inside and out. I got very, very lucky. I could write a full chapter about her so younger men know what to look for, but I'll save that for the next book. Thank you, Erika.

So after dodging a bullet, I'm thinking: *What am I doing? Here's this great person who loved me when I was broke, and she's decent to the core, and I'll never find anyone else like her.*

I make up my mind to get back together—and though she makes me work for it, we finally do.

And now, with the company stable and on a steady upswing, the timing's working out with building a family too. Before, I had no time for anything. Nothing. If I'd had a kid any earlier, the kid would have never seen me. And the second kid probably wouldn't even know what I look like.

Instead, I see them every day. I'm a full-time dad—a *present* dad—which is the most important thing I can be. My son's eight, my daughter's four, and I coach them both in baseball, football, and soccer. I drive them to school, I'm there to give them baths at night, I'm doing exactly what I dreamed of doing. It's amazing.

So this is my life now: family, and continuing to grow Cousins Maine Lobster.

The future? All my life I've been asking the same question—What next?—and I'm young enough that I still do. Maybe it'll be some kind of work in TV. Or, loving sports as much as I do, maybe some sort of cultural marketing position with a local team. I've also thought about getting into politics in Maine.

But all that's for further down the road. For now I just really want to take the time to focus on my family, on my physical and mental health, and on my friends. And to be thankful for all that's happened in the last fourteen years, because, I tell you, it's been a whirlwind.

JIM

Your Little Empire

Back in 2012, when I finally left my old life in Boston behind and moved to LA, I knew only one thing for sure: Cousins Maine Lobster *had* to succeed. And not just as a short-term sensation—it was already that—but as a serious, stable, ongoing enterprise with real potential for growth.

I'd always been a hard worker, goal oriented and highly focused, but I had never been more fully committed to anything in my life. Because there was no alternative, it was either succeed or bust.

I knew it would take relentless effort, and it would go on for as long as it took, and that nothing and no one could stand in its way.

Unfortunately, this was exactly the moment when I fell head over heels in love.

The girl, needless to say, was Maggie.

I knew beforehand that what little social life I'd have in LA (if I had any at all) would not involve ripping around town, going to bars and clubs, looking for random girls. I hoped it might involve the girl I met back in Boston instead.

Even so, that *couldn't* be my highest priority. Our *Shark Tank* segment had been broadcast a month earlier, and between learning the business and getting to know the town, in addition to all the things popping on the publicity front and the possibility of bringing on additional trucks, I was totally swamped.

Still, as soon as I got a moment to breathe, I shot Maggie a text and arranged to get together.

She'd come out west five or six weeks earlier and moved in with her cousin in Hermosa Beach, about forty minutes south of West Hollywood, where I ended up getting my first apartment.

What can I say? Being with her is even better than I could have imagined. From the very start, I mean *instantly*, I'm totally smitten. It's one of those things where as soon as I got home after one of those early dates, I'll immediately call her, then I text her again before going to bed, all the time also worrying that it's pathetic and am I coming on too strong?

But I'm also extremely conscious of the fact that the timing couldn't possibly be worse. Because this is my time to grind. In fact,

I've organized my life around the reality of pretty much devoting my every waking hour to Cousins Maine Lobster.

For one thing, since I no longer have a regular income, I have no money to spend on a girlfriend or much of anything else. Living off my savings, outside of rent, I've taken on no financial responsibilities. I don't have a house or mortgage, and I sure as hell am in no position to take on a wife and kids.

Still, I know I'm probably never going to meet anyone else like this, and so does she. So barely a month after our first date—on November 29, 2012, to be precise—I formally ask her to be my girlfriend over dinner in West Hollywood. This is not a casual thing for either of us; it feels more like a proposal, and that's how we both take it, as a longtime commitment.

But in a way, this complicates things even more. Here she's also just taken a flyer and moved across the country, and now she's stuck with a boyfriend she's hardly ever gonna see. And we both understand this is the way it has to be for as long as it takes.

In practical terms, it means that basically I'm gonna be a hermit. Though she's less than an hour away, I'm almost never gonna have time to drive there. Every day I'll work my face off, go back to my little apartment and make myself dinner, then open my computer and work 'til eleven or midnight.

There'll be long stretches when we probably won't see each other at all. And if we do, it won't be over dinner at a good restaurant. And—outside of a visit to Coachella in a food truck—there definitely won't be time or money for vacations.

But, incredibly, Maggie understands. In fact, more than understand, she *supports* it—both me and this lunatic endeavor we've taken on. From the very beginning, even when the company's the barest gleam of a possibility, when we're starting out with just one truck, she's a believer. She refers to it as "this little empire you're building."

And I'm like, *Yeah, but let's not call it that, okay? Let's not jinx it.*

It's not because I lacked confidence myself—more like, even in hockey, I've never liked claiming success when there's still so much more to do.

It's never lost on me how lucky I am. I mean, I'm working my ass off trying to grow this business, and sometimes things look like they're about to fall apart, and here's someone who never has a moment's doubt.

But, yeah, okay, she's also human. A year into dating, then two and three years into dating, we haven't really moved forward 'cause I've been so busy, and she's starting to wonder if I'm just blowing smoke.

The fact is, even on the rare weekend days I'd make it down to Hermosa Beach, I'd be multitasking, chatting with her as we drove through Hermosa or Manhattan Beach, eyes darting left and right, looking for places I could book the truck, all the time thinking *Does this work; would that? What about that electronics store there, on the corner of the PCH—look how it's jammed with cars on a Saturday!* I mean, that's how I was, always looking, looking, looking for good parking lots.

And those were just regular times. In the bad ones, I *lived* the company in ways I couldn't share with her; experiencing every single twist and turn behind the curtain, the long nightmare of the truck builder crisis, and the pain of the coup. I mean, I'm not gonna run to her with my fucking problems, right—what kind of look is that?

The truth is, there'd be lots of times I was only half there. If we managed a day at the beach, I'm probably lying on my towel reading a fucking eighty-five-page franchise disclosure, page after page of boilerplate, underlining this part in red, scratching out another part, writing a note next to something else. Maybe something about the truck, maybe it's about lobster pricing, who knows, it could be about whether a franchisee can do his own T-shirts. Whatever it is, I've got to make sure I understand every word, so we never get blindsided again.

Meanwhile, Sabin and Shaun, wherever they are, are doing the same thing, so tomorrow we can put all our notes together and give them to our franchise broker, so our thoughts can be input into the doc. I mean, over time we put so much into that damn disclosure doc that by now it's like 350 pages.

And this was my time with Maggie at the beach.

So, yeah, it would be natural for her to start thinking maybe I'm using all the business stuff as an excuse because I'm afraid of commitment. That's what a lot of women would think, right? Or, worse, that deep down I really just don't care enough about her.

Obviously, that's not the case at all—more like the opposite.

At the same time, looking back, it's probably true that I wasn't the kind of guy who'd ever marry a girl I knew just a short time. I'm like my parents that way; I needed to see someone over time and in different circumstances; I needed to see all the nuances. And, really, so did she. In fact, all this time getting to know each other makes our bond a lot stronger than those of most other couples our age.

I remember thinking to myself that she's probably getting an earful from her mother, with whom she's very close. Her mother's a very sweet lady who I really like a lot, but I felt like she didn't understand this whole situation completely. She herself married young to her first husband, Maggie's father, and she's likely sitting there going, *When's this guy gonna propose to you?*

Because that's what you're supposed to do: find the right person to get married to—someone with a good nine-to-five, hopefully the same one for the rest of his life—and raise kids. And, by the way, this is what all Maggie's friends back in Boston are doing. And in fairness, I think my mother felt the same.

What her mother sees is that her daughter is with this guy who's left a very solid, $100K-a-year job for a *food truck*. It certainly wasn't the sexiest story to tell your family about your boyfriend!

Finally, by the end of 2015, we're past the worst of it. The crises have receded and it feels like we have a little breathing space. Things aren't perfect, far from it. But we've got the setup in Maine going, and we're getting a few more trucks on the road, and I'm making some cash—not a lot, but at least enough to go out to better restaurants and to think about starting to save for a ring.

By the following year, November 2016, it's like night and day from where we were just two years before. We're still working nonstop, but the company now has enough healthy franchises to ensure a reliable royalty flow. And with our vetting processes producing a steady stream of strong prospects, and an experienced staff in place to work with them, it's almost like we can snap our fingers and open up another ten any time.

It's been four years since Maggie and I got together. I'm not twenty-seven anymore, I'm thirty-one.

And now I know beyond any question she's the best person in the world, and we have a phenomenal relationship. I can afford to spend money on a ring, and I'm going to propose.

We get married in February 2018.

It is the best and most wonderful day of my life, everything we hoped it would be.

When I make my toast, it's basically a ten-minute ode to Maggie. I share our whole story, starting with that first day I saw her at the hospital. I describe how afterward I tried unsuccessfully to track her down, and how, when I finally found her, she didn't remember me because she'd been hit by a car. I said it was only by the grace of God that I'd bumped into her again, and I was able to reintroduce myself, and we were able to start over. And here we are.

Then I talk about when I first met my mother-in-law and father-in-law, and how it was a little awkward, because what they hear from this guy dating their daughter is that he's just quit his job to open a food truck. Which, let's face it, didn't sound all that great—not like saying I owned a really successful seafood restaurant, or even *two* food trucks.

But because Maggie stuck with me and we kept our heads down and we fought for this business, we made it to where we are.

When Maggie would refer to CML as our "Little Empire," and I never acknowledged it as I didn't want to jinx anything, it was still a very profound and genuine way for her to share her support and belief in me. She was and always has been my biggest reason for doing everything. I think when you find someone in your life who you love unconditionally, and always want to do well and right by, it is that relationship, and meaning, that keeps you on track, keeps you focused and dialed in on making your "thing" work. In my case, my relationship and love for Maggie motivated me and kept me homed in on CML. I knew if we made CML successful it would allow for our relationship to have new opportunies in the future, and for our family to grow in the years to come.

So when she tells me I am building a little empire, the challenge and pressure to make it happen, to see that CML would one day be on its way to that, that just gets even more real. As incredible as our CML team is nationwide, I honestly believe I never would've seen this growth in our business had it not been for the stability that was Maggie. She challenged me, she applauded me, made me think, supported the journey, and more than anything she championed the CML ride with me.

I always remember thinking, if we ever do make this thing a "little empire," my motivation was going to be Maggie, and I'd hope she would relish it as much as I did.

EPILOGUE

The Bottom Line

JIM: So what's the bottom line? After thirteen years, and all the highs and lows of building this company, what have we learned?

Here's my two cents.

The first thing to say is that dealing with it all—the successes but even more so the shitstorms—has made us grow both as partners and as people. We're even closer than we were at the beginning, in fact closer than six or even three years ago. Fewer things get between us or perturb us, the way they did when we were younger. We've been through it all, and not just survived but seen the business grow and prosper, and we just have this tremendous sense of trust in one another. It's not that there are no more problems, or that there won't be bumps in the road, but together we've made it way past that danger zone where there's a chance a business won't work.

SABIN: You'd think that after all this time you might get tired of the other person, because by now you know all his quirks and habits, the good, the bad, and the ugly, and there are partnerships where that might push you away. But in our case it's done the opposite. You have even more respect for the person, you have more empathy for all the things that they're going through, now with wives and kids and life—because I've already gone through so much with this person, so much that's been challenging, where things might've gone south but didn't. And we've grown up together and got past it and gotten way more seasoned.

JIM: Partly it's just a matter of growing in confidence, right? I mean, back when the franchisees staged their coup, we really felt like they might topple us. That would never happen today, because we're very well established now, and we know we've got a brand and a business that works. I don't mean that egotistically; we just know it's our thing, we've been working on it forever, and it's got stability, consistency, recognizability, and meaning.

SABIN: Looking back, facing up to those challenges was essential. If you're going to make it as an entrepreneur, succeed as a dreamer and a builder, you have to go through the trenches. You have to go through that insecurity of being broke, and being exposed, and everything being volatile.

There's no way to circumvent that process. You have to go through those things in order to really appreciate the other side. And it must be really, really lonely to do that alone. But we've had each other.

We also have Shaun, and Barbara, we have our wives and Jim's dad, others we can rely on. But at the end of the day, no one can really understand like Jim and I can what it's taken to get here, because it's just a different level of dedication.

JIM: Sabe's the one who from the beginning was big on building the culture. My focus was more on the business. But I quickly learned that culture is everything. If you have a great culture, if you have a great team, good people, everything else flows from that. When it all comes together—the right people, the right markets—it's gonna work. The opportunities are endless.

SABIN: And you can't cut corners in those relationships any more than you can in your personal life. It's like my relationship with my wife. We've had ups, we've had downs, we've had unexpected twists and turns, but you never stop nurturing it, and now we're closer than ever. It's the same with our staff and our franchisees and our other business partners.

There's no way to fast-forward life. But if you do things the right way and you really care, you will get the positive results. And I think that that's something the younger generation doesn't want to do. They just want to become rich. But you have to be true to yourself and your values.

JIM: One thing I'm really thankful for now that we have a successful established business is that we get to help other people in really meaningful ways. I like to tell the story of the guy, Gavin, that I hired a few years ago from a Christmas tree lot in Massachusetts. This kid was working there, shoveling trees onto people's cars. He recognized the Cousins Maine Lobster coat I was wearing and we started talking.

He told me he worked for a soccer team in New York, doing their marketing and sales, knocking on doors and giving out stickers and flyers, and he probed me about our business. He was just very eloquent and engaged, and I could see his work ethic and hustle. So, I hired him three years ago. Now he's probably one of our top-five employees.

He just got engaged and we sent him a bottle of Dom Pérignon, because I remember being that age and being like, *Holy shit, I'm never gonna buy a bottle of Dom.* He called and he's like, *Thank you for giving me this chance.* And I said to him, like, *Dude, it's all you.*

Because really I was just paying it back, like my owners at Stryker who gave me a shot at that age. Yeah, we could have been dicks, we could have taken every dollar from the business and put it in our pocket, but that was never our mentality.

You know, all that time we were working nonstop on the company, everything else took a back seat. Whereas now other things have become, I don't want to say more important, but of course, your kids and your wife really are. So it's almost like a crazy little skill in and of itself to have them kind of coexist in a way that each benefits the other.

Because family *is* everything. You know, Sabe's mom and my mom and dad, it's like every fucking week there's someone in their lives who's sick or dying, and it's terrible. And it reminds you, as if you need reminding, of what really matters. And one of the ways we're blessed is that this is truly a family business. Our parents are proud of it, our wives are proud of it, our kids are proud of it . . .

SABIN: I was in the car the other day with my son. I'd taken him golfing for the first time in his life, and he actually paid attention and tried hard, which if you know him, is astounding. Because he's like me, really quick to move on from things.

So we're on the road home, and we're on like this natural high, and he's already asking when we can play again, and five blocks from my house there's a CML truck parked and serving. He saw it and begged me to pull over and I was saying no because we were really late, but he begged and begged and begged. So we pull over, and he goes to talk to the person, and he says, "My dad is Sabin Lomac, he's one of the cousins." And he was so proud.

Then he went on the truck and he made a lobster roll and took it home and actually ate it, and I didn't think he really liked lobster, but he wolfed it down. And it was one of the top-ten moments of my life.

JIM: My daughters Olive and Coco have really been picking up on what I do and what CML is all about. When I go to grand openings, they want to go. When I go to the office, they ask if I'm going to "work on Cousins Maine Lobster." I could've stayed at Stryker, and of course Olive and Coco would have been proud. But when you create something of your own, and when your kids can then look and go, "That's Daddy on the screen!" or that truck rolling down the street is the brainchild of my dad, that's a really special thing to share with them, or a legacy to leave behind.

Olive and Coco love being in Maine during the summer, going on lobster boats, hauling up traps and banding lobsters. They realize where the resource begins, and how it goes to CML trucks throughout the country. And now it's gotten to the point where they both look forward to having steamed lobsters in the summer, picking the meat from the knuckles and claws, and appreciating the delicacy that lobster is, and that is the foundation of our business. Does it sound familiar? I get to smile and always think of my mom and Aunt Jeannie when I see my daughters picking their way through a steamed lobster.

SABIN: When we were in Italy this past April for Easter, we were on our way to Vatican City to get some rosary beads to pay our respects—this was right after the pope died—and my son turned to me and said, "Dad, when are you gonna retire from Cousins Maine Lobster?"

I said, "I don't know, I have no plans."

"Well, who's gonna do your job when you retire?"

And I said, "I don't know. Do you have any suggestions?"

And he goes, "Me. Dad, I wanna do it."

I smiled so big that Erika, my wife, told me she'd never seen me happier.

ACKNOWLEDGMENTS

Our parents: Julie, Steve, and Jeannie
Our amazing wives: Maggie and Erika
Our children: Enzo, Isla, Olive, and Coco
Our rocks: Shaun Higgins and Jameson Lyons
Our amazing partner and mentor: Barbara Corcoran
Our families: Lomac and Tselikis
Our adopted sharks: Daymond John and Robert Herjavec
Our representation: Diane Perez, Scott Kaufman, and Cheryl Crowley
Our champions: Clay Newbill, Yun Lingner, and Mindy Zemrak
Our voice: Harry Stein
Our home: The beautiful state of Maine
Our core: The entire Cousins Maine Lobster family

ABOUT THE AUTHORS

Raised in Scarborough, Maine, SABIN LOMAC grew up a stone's throw from a working waterfront, where lobster traps line the docks and the local economy centers around lobster. Growing up in a single-parent household, with his loving mom, Jeannie, Sabin quickly developed an appreciation for both family and the traditions that bring families together. After being crowned the "man of the house" at a young age, Sabin went to work and hasn't stopped yet. He learned that hard work, though not always pretty, will always win in the end.

In 2012, Sabin, along with his cousin, Jim, appeared on ABC's hit show *Shark Tank*, where the cousins partnered with real estate mogul and business auteur Barbara Corcoran. Since then, Cousins Maine Lobster has grown into a nationwide brand, with food trucks and restaurants bringing wild-caught Maine lobster to unique neighborhoods across the nation.

Sabin is a proud husband to Erika, and a loving father to Enzo and Isla.

Jim Tselikis grew up in Cape Elizabeth, Maine, a prominent headland that marks the southern entrance to Casco Bay, and is home to the Portland Head Light, the most famous lighthouse in the world. From its rocky shores one can see a bustling community of lobster boats fishing Casco Bay's rich waters, and colorful lobster buoys dotting the coastline. From an early age, Jim was immersed in traditions that defined the region's coastal culture, helping his parents Julie and Steve steam bounties of Maine lobsters for family gatherings and holidays. Gathering around wooden picnic tables with the summer Maine sun shining, Jim and his family would sit, drenched up to their elbows in buttery Maine lobster.

These early experiences sparked a passion in Jim, not only for great seafood but for family, tradition, and the hardworking communities that make it all possible. Guided by a commitment to quality, community, and shared experiences, Jim founded Cousins Maine Lobster with his cousin Sabin, focusing on growing the business while staying true to the traditions that inspire it.

In 2012 after Cousins Maine Lobster was birthed, Jim and his cousin Sabin appeared on ABC's hit show *Shark Tank*, where they partnered with Barbara Corcoran. Since then, Cousins Maine Lobster has grown to 100 units nationwide and with more to come.

Jim is a loving husband to Maggie, and a proud father to Olive and Coco.